BEFORE THE WINDS
OF CHANGE

A catalogue record of this book is available from the British
Library

First Edition: December 2004

ISBN: 1-84375-124-0

To order additional copies of this book please visit:
http://www.upso.co.uk/frankglynn

Published by: UPSO Ltd
5 Stirling Road, Castleham Business Park,
St Leonards-on-Sea, East Sussex TN38 9NW United Kingdom
Tel: 01424 853349 Fax: 0870 191 3991
Email: info@upso.co.uk Web: http://www.upso.co.uk

To John

With best wishes and
warmest regards.

Frank.

BEFORE THE WINDS
OF CHANGE

A
MEMOIR OF COLONIAL SERVICE
IN TANGANYIKA

By
Frank Glynn, OBE

UPSO

Dedication

This memoir is dedicated to my wife, Wyn and
to my children Margaret, Peter, Philip and Fiona
and to all my grandchildren.

The story is written as I remember the different episodes without
embroidery. In some cases the names have been changed but the
circumstances described are as best as I can remember them.

Frank Glynn

Table of Contents

PART 1

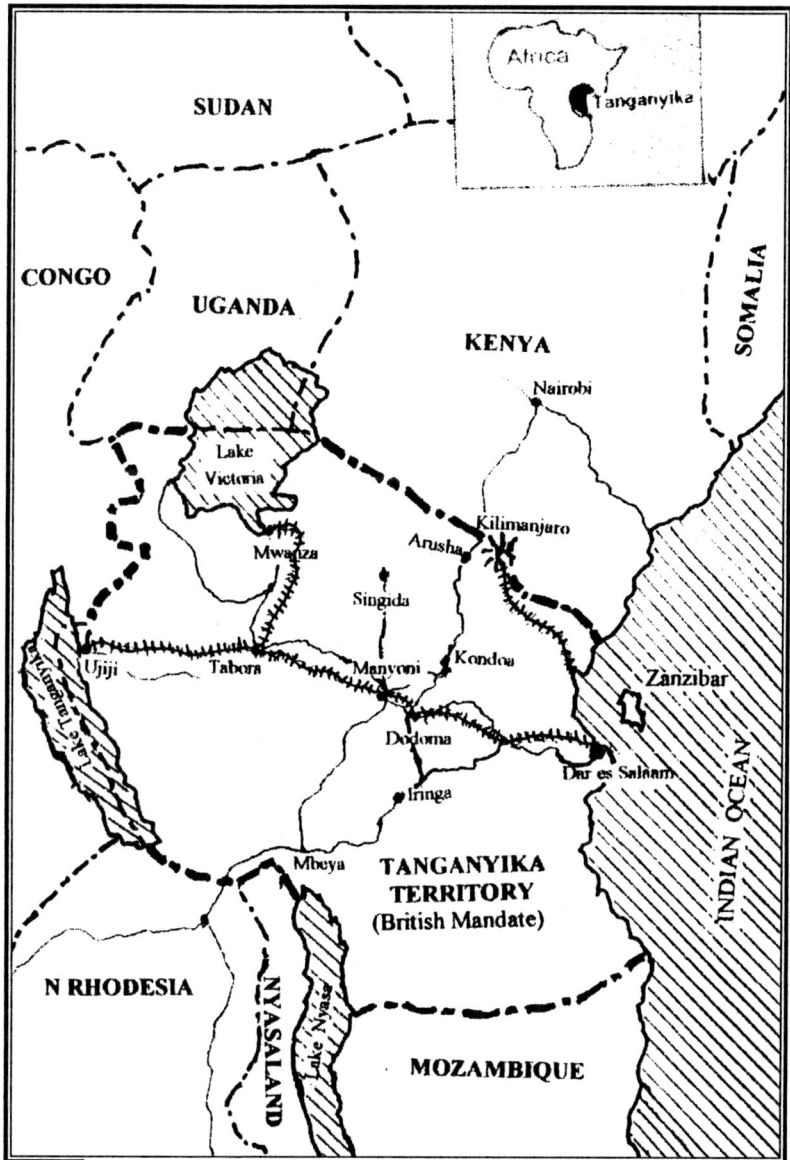

APPOINTMENT AND EMBARKATION

Leaving the Army to join the Colonial Service was something of a challenge, however, with many Regiments being amalgamated, including my own, and with some 400 surplus Majors blighting promotion prospects, as a Captain and Adjutant a new career choice seemed advisable. At the age of 35 with a wife and young family I was too young to plateau so, in seeking suitable alternative employment, I applied to the Colonial Office for an overseas appointment. My subsequent interview at the Colonial Appointments Board seemed to be based entirely on my ability to discuss the issues set out in the editorial page of that day's edition of the Times. Fortuitously, and most unusually, I had read a copy of the Times, which someone had left in the train, as I was travelling to the interview. Salary, promotion prospects, duties and responsibilities, etc. were not discussed but there seemed to be a worrying assumption that I possessed some form of private income. The only unequivocal assurance I received was to the effect that if I were fortunate enough to survive to the age of 55 I could expect to retire on full pension – subsequent events were to reveal that there were no grounds for such optimism. Almost as an afterthought one member of the Board asked if I would be comfortable working with Africans and this seemed to be the only job related question throughout the discussion. On leaving the interview room I stepped into a lift which was occupied by Africans, very large, very black, sporting an impressive array of facial tribal scars and engaged in an animated discussion in some form of tribal dialect. It struck me that if the noise had been coming from anyone else there would have been good grounds for assuming that they were desperately ill. On leaving my Regiment my Colonel's advice, on dealing with Africans, was to treat them exactly the same as one would treat anyone else. This encounter seemed to be an excellent opportunity to put this advice to the test; accordingly, I promptly ignored them.

My acceptance of a subsequent offer of a probationary appointment, on terms and conditions which seemed to be an improvement on my present arrangements, resulted in an active scramble in which our household effects were packed in crates ready for shipment. The house closed down, children removed from school, inoculations for the whole family arranged and farewells to our families and friends all taken care of in quick time. The sea voyage from London to Dar es Salaam, Tanganyika, via Suez, was an adventure greatly anticipated by the whole family, my wife Wyn and our three children Margaret, Peter and Philip. We embarked on a Union Castle ship berthed in the King George the V dock in London under somewhat chaotic circumstances. The Dock Workers Union had called a strike and hemmed in the ship with Lighters to prevent it leaving the dockside. However, the Captain was determined to sail on the tide and his not too sensitive manoeuvring caused a fair amount of damage to the Lighters and the port installations as a consequence. The ship's departure was further aggravated by the actions of the strikers who had loaded all the passengers baggage in one great heap on the forward deck with Hold and Cabin baggage intermixed. Many passengers spent their time sailing down the Thames estuary searching over the pile trying to locate their cabin baggage; the convention that passengers did not dress for dinner on the first night of the voyage was not an option in this case.

Notwithstanding the uncertain start, the voyage certainly matched our expectations but we could have been more comfortable had we been able to travel in First Class in accordance with my travel entitlement. However, the Crown Agents passages department claimed that First Class was fully booked and, since the Tanganyika authorities had stipulated that I was required immediately in Dar es Salaam, a tourist passage would have to be accepted. On my arrival in Dar es Salaam there was no evidence of any anxiety that I should take up an immediate appointment and in subsequent discussions with experienced officers it became clear that this was standard treatment for officers on first appointment. It is questionable whether the modest savings on the Crown agents travel budget could really be justified bearing in mind the resentment built up amongst serving officers and their families who regarded this policy as little short of sharp practice. Experienced officers confronted with arguments of this kind would simply refuse to travel until a passage at the correct grade level could be found. The voyage out was something we had all been looking forward to and it certainly came up to our expectations. Gibraltar and the Mediterranean with a short stop in Genoa before reaching Port Said and Suez proved to be fascinating, although some elderly passengers who doubtless had made this journey on previous occasions treated our pleasure and amazement with scarcely hidden contempt. Long before we reached Gibraltar the passengers seemed to have sorted themselves out into a well defined pecking order based on the Passenger List circulated by the Pursers Office. This was carefully studied in a manner peculiar to the English at sea and a sort of precedence was worked out particularly amongst the Colonial Service passengers, bridge sets were agreed and seating arrangements at tables in the dining saloon were quietly established through negotiations with the Chief Steward. Overall, the passengers appeared to fall naturally into three distinct groups, the Colonial service where honours and awards or seniority were accorded the respect to which at least the holders considered to be justified. The second group was largely made up of what might loosely be described as the 'Commercials' general managers and professional staff of major commercial undertakings – generally more affluent and likely to congregate in the various bars and lounges often till late evening in an atmosphere of fiesta. Finally, there were the Missionaries, the priests and lay-brothers with a fair sprinkling of nuns, teachers and nurses, often to be found holding ad-hoc prayer meetings in various parts of the ship interspersed with lessons in Swahili for those on first appointment. These were the most abstemious group on board as Wyn discovered to her consternation during an incident in which one of the Lay Sisters collapsed due to heat exhaustion as we sailed through the Red Sea. Wyn sought to help by offering a sip of brandy but this was a kindness which was seriously resented when the Lay Sister recovered. Apparently, she had a life-long commitment to avoid the demon alcohol in any form and had the feeling she had been taken advantage of.

A very worrying situation developed as we entered the Indian Ocean en-route to Mombasa. Our son Peter suddenly developed chronic groin pains and the ship's doctor seemed to be at a loss in diagnosing the problem. Despite the fact that Peter was in real pain he suggested the problem was quite superficial and would probably go away given time. As the problem continued and seemed to get worse he even suggested that Peter was making a fuss unnecessarily. As the pain got worse and Peter was perspiring, unable to eat and clearly dehydrating, I consulted the ship's Captain with a view to getting Peter to the nearest port, Mogadishu. Since we were only 28 hours from Mombasa the Captain's view was that it would probably be better to get help there as the medical facilities in Somalia were to say the least uncertain. He also thought that it might be possible to find a doctor amongst the passengers who could give a second opinion.

In the event a missionary medical aid was found who, though experienced as a medical technician, was clearly afraid of being seen to interfere with the ship's doctor's patient. By now Peter was taking liquids and his temperature had dropped slightly although the pain returned spasmodically and he was still confined to his bunk. It wasn't until we got him admitted to hospital on arrival in Dar es Salaam that the problem was properly diagnosed and an immediate operation arranged accordingly. These events overshadowed all other issues as we disembarked and it was only after we were assured that Peter was in good hands that we were able to react to our new situation in Dar es Salaam.

PART 2

FIRST NIGHT IN AFRICA

Contrary to information provided by the Crown Agents, it was soon evident that my presence in Tanganyika was not urgently required. Notwithstanding the six weeks notice the Department must have had of my departure from London it was obvious that my arrival was something of a surprise. Timely reservations had not been booked for us in any of the usual hotels and these in the event were all fully booked. As a temporary measure we were informed that we would have to stay in a little used hotel across the harbour accessible only by a battered wooden motor launch manned by an African crew. As we scrambled aboard and tried to make sure our baggage did not fall into the oily bilge water swilling about in the bottom of the boat we were able to take some account of our surroundings. In the hot bright sunshine and clear blue water we were able to see that the palm fringed harbour really lived up to its name – Dar es Salaam – Haven of Peace. The peace was short lived, however, as the engine of the launch caught fire half way across the harbour. The crew seemed to react to the situation as a matter of course. The engine was switched off and then doused with water from the bilges until the flames had been extinguished, we were then rowed the rest of the journey eventually scrambling ashore on to a rickety landing stage. The hotel itself seemed idyllic, located on a clean, palm fringed sandy beach overlooking the harbour entrance with a panoramic view of the Zanzibar Channel. However, we were warned not to drink the water as there was no mains supply on this side of the harbour and such as was available came from a nearby well which was contaminated by sea water and was regarded as a serious health hazard. The hotel was a medium sized building of modern cement block construction and well designed but we were the only residents doubtless due to the contaminated water and an uncertain power supply. Our accommodation on the first floor with a balcony overlooking the harbour was really comfortable with clean mosquito nets over each bed and en-suite facilities which were much better than we had been led to expect. Our first night in Africa was a constant surprise, it was dark by 6.30 when, due to a power cut, Tilley lamps were lit and every kind of creepy crawley emerged. Insects of various shapes and sizes gathered round the lamps and 'Geckos' (small almost transparent lizards) ran about the walls and ceilings licking up insects with their long tongues. What we came to recognize later as hunting spiders, about three inches long with formidable antlers, shot across the floor mopping up moths which had had been attracted to the lamps and perished as a consequence. For the first time we experienced the background noises of a tropical African night, a constant racket from insects, mosquitoes, frogs, and other nameless creatures and bats flying about on the balcony. Notwithstanding the heat and humidity, it was reassuring to be safely tucked up in bed protected by our mosquito nets. Sleep was not easily achieved with thoughts of Peter and my new appointment uppermost in my mind and when I finally drifted off a sudden noise on the balcony woke me with a jerk. When I reached the balcony door to investigate an African was making his escape over the balcony wall to disappear into the darkness – the first but by no means the our only experience of African thieves.

The Department's headquarters were located almost opposite the hotel on the other side of the harbour and consisted of single storied thatched roofed buildings arranged round a central quadrangle within the welcome shade of palm trees. I was met on arrival by the Assistant Labour Commissioner who proved to be helpful and friendly particularly when we discovered that we both came from the north of England. He introduced me to the Headquarters staff, the key meeting of which was with the Labour Commissioner. He indicated that he ran the Department on military lines and that I should see the Department as a Divisional Headquarters with himself as the presiding General, his Deputy as possibly a half Colonel and the Assistant Commissioner at the level of Brigade Major. The twenty or so Labour Officers which I would be joining were out-posted to the Provinces and, though all graded at the same level, they were paid differently according to their length of service. In a relatively short time I was able to put this Ruritanian concept into a more realistic perspective bearing in mind that the Departments total Establishment was less than 300 employees most of whom were Asian middle level or African subordinate staff. Ranking the Commissioner at the level Colonel and the rest adjusted accordingly seemed to be more closely in line with the actuality. I was shortly to learn that the Commissioner was not known for underestimating his own importance; when frustrated even over minor issues he would describe himself as a race horse pulling coal cart. This seemed to do little for the moral of the Headquarters staff who appeared to be well adjusted to his egocentric behaviour but treated him with a fair amount of caution nevertheless.

I had been informed by the Colonial Office that my first assignment would be to Mwanza on Lake Victoria after a short period of induction training at Headquarters. The training started when the Assistant Labour Commissioner suggested that I should read through the various Acts and Regulations which provided the statutory frame-work within which the Department operated. I was also informed that I would be required to pass Advanced Level Kiswahili written and oral examinations as well as Law Examinations within two years if my probationary status was to be converted into a permanent appointment. Sitting alone at a table confronted by a formidable stack of legislation I was greatly distracted by a magnificent view through the open window of the palm fringed harbour and the cries of African fishermen sailing through the harbour entrance returning from a nights fishing. Their voices carried clearly across the water as they paddled in to the sandy beach in their dug-out canoes loaded with a strange variety of colourful tropical fish. I had scarcely opened the first volume of the Laws before The Assistant Commissioner returned to inform me that my assignment to Mwanza had been cancelled and that I was to take up an appointment as Labour Officer, Central Province. I was to be stationed at the Provincial Headquarters in Dodoma and it was essential that I move immediately. Induction training seemed to have been forgotten as arrangements were put in hand for me and the family, less Peter who was still in hospital, to board the next train up the Central

Line. I was concerned with checking out of the hotel, making arrangements for my baggage to be cleared by the Landing and Shipping Agents and moving the family up to Dodoma by train as soon as possible. Apparently this sudden move was necessary because the Labour Officer I would be relieving was in need of medical attention which was only available in Dar es Salaam, hence the sudden change of plan. Leaving Peter alone in hospital was our immediate concern, but we were assured that he would be well looked after by people in the Department and that he would be flown up to join us in Dodoma as soon as it was safe to discharge him from hospital. When this was explained to Peter he did not seem too concerned as he was obviously fairly comfortable in hospital and the medical staff and other patients in his ward were keeping a kindly eye on him. Boarding the train in Dar es Salaam was something of a shambles, the platform was crowded with people, mostly Africans, and keeping an eye on our baggage was not easy. Porters literally came to blows as they fought to carry our baggage on to the train in anticipation of a tip. We were pleasantly surprised at the high standard of accommodation in the train as we shared two adjoining First Class Coupes with comfortable seats, washing facilities, electric fans and mosquito nets. The journey from the coast up to Dodoma is about 320 miles and normally takes two days as the train stops at regular intervals to take on fuel and water. The train moved at a leisurely pace through the outskirts of Dar es Salaam and into the African bush, passing through small villages of traditional African huts made from local materials. Passing through these the train's whistle was constantly sounding to alert children, cattle and goats on or too close to the line. As we moved inland across the coastal plain the land was green and seemingly productive as we passed through shambas in which maize, millet and sorghum were growing and coconut palms, bananas, mangoes and paw-paw were much in evidence near the villages. About thirty miles inland the train started the gradual climb up on to the Nyika, the more or less flat plain about 3 to 4 thousand feet above sea level, which is typical of most parts of Tanganyika – in Swahili the name Tanganyika takes its name from the coastal town of Tanga and the 'nyika' which lies inland from there. From time to time the train rattled over bridges spanning dry riverbeds and eventually the land deteriorated into dry desert like scrubland with thick thorn bush close up to the train line. From time to time there would be open Savannah interspersed with Baobab trees, Euphorbia cacti like bushes and Acacia and Miombo trees; all very different to what we were used to. Our eyes were glued to the bush notwithstanding as we expected to see some sign of African wildlife. After hours of careful watching we were finally rewarded by the sight of a bunch of baboon seemingly waiting to cross the line.

Dinner was signaled by a servant passing along the train corridor beating a gong and inviting us to the dining car. Walking through the train we passed the kitchen in which the cooks were busy over a smoky wood burning stove preparing our evening meal in conditions which didn't look at all promising. However, we were pleasantly surprised to find that an excellent meal was served by cheerful and friendly African staff in a very modern dining car with ice cold gin and tonic and the ubiquitous Coca-Cola. By then it was dark but the train was well lit and, on our returning to our compartments we found the top bunks had been folded down and our bedrolls and mosquito nets all set in place ready for the night. It was now noticeably cooler and we welcomed the sheets and blankets as we snuggled in our bunks safe from the dreaded mosquitoes. Our last thoughts were with Peter, alone in the hospital in Dar es Salaam, hoping he was well and knowing how much he would have enjoyed the adventure of such a train journey. The next morning was interesting but uneventful and after a good breakfast and lunch the train arrived in Dodoma more or less on time in the late afternoon. We were met on arrival by the officer I was due to replace. Eventually we would be allocated his house after he had packed his belongings and moved on to Dar es Salaam. Under his kindly guidance we spent a few days adjusting to our new life in the Colonial Service. Wyn coming to terms with running a house with African servants (the kitchen had a wood burning stove and was located about twenty yards behind the house so a cook was essential) and settling the children into the local school. She was introduced to the neighbouring expatriate wives and had to learn the arcane business of shopping at the local Asian owned shops (dukas) whose printed bills, with good reason, carried the unequivocal message that 'No Goods Were Guaranteed'. I was busy taking over the Department, meeting the staff, checking the stores and accounts and being formally introduced to the senior officials normally to be found in a Provincial Headquarters. The reactions at different levels was quite interesting, the most senior officers friendly and welcoming whilst at the lower levels the responses were more speculatively appraising – first appointment, new to Africa, no experience and in some cases 'no hoper' seemed to be the scarcely hidden conclusion. Only one person, the Resident Magistrate, seemed to feel that he had a duty to put me in my place by advancing the following advice- 'You have to realize right at the outset that everybody who is anybody round here will probably see you as an enemy. Since they all, in one way or another, employ African labour and its your responsibility to see that their terms of employment are fair and reasonable so you can never expect them to fully accept you. This is particularly the case with women whose role as employers of African servants often give rise to problems and they cannot easily accept that you will support African complaints when dealing with disputes over wages or behaviour. You can be as neutral as you wish but you will be seen as an 'African Lover' who cannot be relied upon to see the difficulties which can arise from employing dishonest or idle Africans'. I soon came to realise that this unsettling piece of gratuitous advice was best ignored. Subsequent events were to prove that there was very little substance in these views and in reality I was to find that in the most difficult labour disputes the assistance of Labour Officers was greatly valued and much sought after. I also came to realise that racial discord along these lines was largely a feature of the Magistrates own attitude to race relations. It was ironic that I was subsequently obliged to take a case against him for failing to pay wages to his African cook, one of the rare occasions when I was unable to settle a dispute without resort to the court.

The house we were allocated proved surprisingly comfortable contra to all our expectations. A modern three bed-roomed bungalow with a spacious lounge, modern bathroom and toilet, and an open veranda overlooking a specious garden bordered by a thick Manyara hedge. Some twenty yards behind the house were the kitchen and the servants quarters. The hot water system depended on a large wood burning fire-place located at the side of the house over the top of which was a 44 gallon water drum under which a fire was kept burning during the day time. The house was equipped with good basic furniture the standard of which we discovered was governed by ones grade in the service. Even at my grade it was perfectly adequate and once our baggage arrived Wyn was able to make the place quite comfortable. The house was located on the outer fringe of the European part of the town south of the railway line to the north of which was the commercial centre and the Asian residential area and beyond that the African township constructed mainly of traditional materials.

Because of our location on the edge of the residential area close to the adjoining bush, our dustbins were first to receive the attention of hyenas which invaded the town as soon as it was dark. Because the dam which supplied the town's water was less than a mile away from the house, it was possible but rare to hear lions roaring as they came in to drink at the dam during the night. Leopards were the other more frequent nocturnal visitors seemingly because they were particularly partial to dogs of which there were a fair number in the expatriate quarter. Early evidence of this was provided by one of our neighbours who owned a pair of dachshund dogs. On returning from a late shift at about 2am he drove up to the house only to find a pair of fullygrown leopards sprawled across his veranda blocking his front door. He was obliged to remain in his car for ages until they deigned to move away, if he sounded his horn his wife would come to the front door and the dogs would race out and that would be the end of the dogs – if not the wife.

The officer I was relieving was helpful when it came to hiring servants, a new experience for us. Sam, hired as a cook on the basis of a rather scruffy collection of 'chits' from previous employers, was a man in his late forties, although his age was difficult to judge. His cheerful smile was somewhat compromised by his possession of a full set of sharply filed teeth which, together with tribal facial scars and a very black skin indicated that he came from somewhere in the Lake region. Joseph, hired as a

'House-Boy', was a member of the local Wagogo tribe, small in stature with a light brown complexion and Nilotic, as opposed to Bantu features, had a 'chit' that indicated that he 'worked well under supervision'. He would clean the house, do the laundry and ironing, serve the meals, make the beds and do the washing up. Finally, there was Juma, hired as a 'Shamba Boy', also an Mgogo, who would undertake gardening duties and chop wood for the fires under the hot water tank and the kitchen stove. None of them spoke English of course but they all had previous experience of their duties having worked for other European families. Communicating with the servants was based on a certain amount of inspired sign language and frequent resort to our bible – Bishop Steeres Kiswahili Grammar – but this had its limitations since they mostly spoke Chigogo as their tribal language and resorted to a sort of kitchen swahili as the best option. The outcome of all this led to some strange and often hilarious situations but fairly soon some sort of modus vivendi was arrived at which gradually improved as our knowledge of swahili improved. At first it seemed simpler to watch the servants perform their duties, since they rather than we, had a clearer understanding of what should be done and this worked out pretty well. Under these arrangements the house was cleaned, floors were polished, beds made, laundry gathered and washed and ironed, tables laid for meals, dishes washed, all as a matter of course. Water was a real problem as the stuff that emerged from the tap was often the colour of weak cocoa and had to be filtered and boiled before cooking or drinking. As the dry season continued and the level of the dam fell this could only get worse and the hope was that good rains would eventually lead to an improvement.

Sam proved to be a surprisingly good cook considering that he was operating on a primitive wood stove and we would be astonished when from time to time he would produce beautifully light souffles and good chicken curries. Food, however, was another matter and Wyn had to keep a very wary eye on this at all times. An account was opened with Remtullah's an Asian owned general store (duka) in the commercial part of the town. The need for vigilance was ever present as things like sugar, flour cereals etc. had to be sieved to remove grubs and insects. But canned goods were reliable albeit expensive. Milk, when available, was often sour and contained a kind of grey sludge which was pretty off-putting so canned powdered – milk became the norm. Fresh meat was another matter. The only butcher in the town was a Greek who would buy a beast at the local cattle market and kill it on open ground by the side of his shop. The skinned carcass would then be hung in a large fly screened meat safe as the whole shop was alive with flies. Butchering was something less than a fine art as, having been told how much meat was required, the Greek would open the meat safe and take a swing at the carcass with a large very sharp knife. He dropped the results on to the scales until the right weight was achieved. During this process flies would swarm into the meat safe until it sometimes seemed that there were more flies in the safe than in the shop. So, unless someone had shot some game on safari, fresh meat was avoided in favour of canned. The butcher also served something which he described as 'boys meat' whose provenance was a bit worrying although it didn't bother the servants who cheerfully accepted this as part of their weekly rations; there was something else which he described as 'dog meat' which didn't stand thinking about. An alternative was local hens or chickens brought to the house live by vendors and allowed to run around in the garden until required for a meal. The Swahili name for a chicken is 'cuckoo' which caused some confusion at first, but whatever it was called, when cooked it usually turned out to be a collection of bones joined together by strong elastic. Eggs too were readily available which again were brought round to the house by local Africans and Sam would test each one by floating them in a bowl of water the floaters being rejected as too old. So our domestic life seemed to settle down to a fairly simple routine although we were frequently reminded that we were operating in a fairly primitive environment. Philip, our three year old son, once entered the house pulling a length of string on the end of which was a fluttering beautiful red-breasted starling. Sam had caught it, broken its wings, and given it to Philip to play with; he was genuinely puzzled at our horrified reactions.

TAKING OVER THE DEPARTMENT

I had been introduced briefly to the staff at the Department but it was now time to start my new role as Provincial Labour Officer and assume responsibility for the Departments activities. On his departure my predecessor had said 'Don't worry, everything is in the files'; it was now time to put this optimistic view to the test. It was always a pleasure to walk down from the house to the office at 7.30 in the morning in clear bright warm sunshine under a cloudless sky. With cape doves calling in the background and a dawn chorus of bird song, crickets chirping and the scuttering of large purple necked lizards in the dried leaves in the monsoon ditches alongside the road, there couldn't have been a more pleasant start to the day. At first I greeted everyone I met with the comment 'What a nice day'. This invariably invoked startled looks and some surprise since I had yet to learn that in the Central Province it was always a warm beautiful morning except on those uncertain occasions when the rains came.

The Department was housed in a modern cement block single storey building with a corrugated sheet metal roof sited on a dusty patch of sandy soil close to the Provincial Headquarters (the Boma). The building was divided into my office with a store attached, the main office housing the filing system and presided over by Mr. Panjawani the Asian Chief Clerk / Accountant assisted by Mr. Johnathan an African typist. Another office was occupied by Aron Nyrenda, the African Labour Inspector, who dealt with most complaints in the first instance. There was a smaller room used by the messengers, supervised unofficially by Maloda, who claimed the non-existent title of 'Head Messenger'. All the rooms were linked by a veranda running across the front of the building. On the western edge of the town was a Labour Transit Centre and Dispensary manned by an Overseer / Dresser and three Sweepers – a similar Centre was located at Itigi about 80 miles west of Dodoma on the Central railway line.

It all seemed a long way from the Regimental Headquarters to which I was accustomed, not least because of the overall scruffy appearance of everything from the battered sign over the front entrance to the unkempt area surrounding the building. Inside the concrete floors were dirty and un-swept, files seemed to be piled all over the place and the eaves and corners of the roof and ceilings were thick with spiders webs. A major effort would have to be made to get the place up to an acceptable standard. It was also clear that something would have to be done about the area outside of the building on which a crowd of Africans were usually crouched or lying waiting to register their complaints or seeking information about employment opportunities. This area was littered with the chewed remnants of sugar cane, mango and banana skins, rubbish of all kinds and fly ridden as a consequence. Regarding the staff, it would obviously take some time to reach an understanding of their functions and abilities and it may also take some time to secure their confidence and cooperation. The period of familiarisation would obviously work both ways and I was very conscious of the fact that I, (a very white skinned, blue eyed, fair-haired European who didn't speak Swahili) was being closely observed by everyone although they all appeared to be friendly and helpful. At the administrative level much depended on Mr. Panjawani who had been in post for over nine years and whose administrative memory of the operations of the Department was going to be a key element in maintaining continuity. He was a very short, slightly overweight, dark skinned Hindu in his mid fifties, with a house and large family in the Asian quarter. According to his confidential report, he had an extensive net-work of contacts in the Asian community where he was well respected and he was a reliable and competent accountant. The filing system, such as it was seemed to be mainly in Mr. Panjawani's head and whilst he could comfortably find his way about the files nobody else could. He suffered from an acute adenoidal complaint which, combined with his accent, made his speech difficult to understand. This meant that one had to listen to him very closely but since he was invariably reeking of garlic this was not always easy. Despite his sombre expression he was friendly enough although he was seldom seen to smile and his attitude to the subordinate staff, who he clearly didn't trust, struck me as pretty aggressive. He would seldom volunteer information or comment but would respond helpfully to any inquiries.

Aron Nyrenda, the Labour Inspector, was a straightforward individual who in his military service had held the rank of sergeant in the Kings African Rifles. He took a pride in his turnout, the buttons of his khaki tunic and cap badge were always well polished and he was seldom seen without his solar topee. He was an Mnyasa by tribe, having been born in Nyasaland, but he had a family with him in Dodoma. In appearance he was quite

Staff at the Department
Panjawani on my right and Aron on my left.
Back row, Elio, Abdullah, Jonathon and Maloda.

different to the people in the local Wagogo tribe, tall, well built, a very black skin and the thick lips typical of the Bantu tribes south of East Africa. As I got to know him I wondered if his father may have been Nigerian since many served as troops fighting the Germans in the 1914-18 war in East Africa. Like many people in Nyasaland he was a staunch Christian having been educated up to Standard 10 in one of the Livingstone Missionary Schools – hence his good command of English. His primary function was to deal with complaints in the first instance and he had a reputation for being fair and honest, but with little admiration for the local Wagogo tribe. He would also accompany me on Labour and Factory Inspections throughout the Province.

Mr. Johnathan, whose second name was almost unpronounce-able, had recently left school at the age of 20 and still dressed in his school uniform. White shirt and shorts plus a very battered pair of black shoes at least two sizes too big for him; these he invariably removed when he was in the office. He was still trying to come to terms with the typewriter but compensated for this by his ability to spell or more often to correct my spelling. He had an engaging smile and seemed to regard everything that was happening in the Department as mildly amusing. His ambition in life was to play professional football and he could hardly wait for the office to close so that he could join his team in the evening.

The three Messengers were all Wagogo and very typical of their tribe. Small in build with brown as opposed to black skin and Nilotic features which they claimed related them to the neighbouring Masai tribe although the Masai would strongly deny this. There wasn't an ounce of fat on any of them, a reflection of the poor food choices typically available in the semi-desert conditions of the Central Province. Each had the distinctive Gogo tribal marking on their foreheads just above the bridge of the nose. This was caused by placing a red-hot piece of charcoal on their foreheads during their initiation ceremony; the bigger the scar the better the man apparently. They all had long extended ear lobes weighted down with copper ear rings or wooden plugs. Their uniform was a simple short sleeved khaki tunic, a pair of khaki shorts and a red fez. To distinguish them

from other Messengers in Government service they wore a brass
badge on their left breast with the words Department of Labour
engraved on it. Shoes were not issued and bare feet seemed to be
the norm. Like most Wagogo each of them carried a 'Panga' of
Gogo design – a two foot wooden handle into which was fitted a
ten inch sharp steel blade. This was used for everything from
cutting toe nails, chopping wood etc. and, usually when drunk
each other. Maloda set himself up as the natural leader of this
group constantly issuing orders and generally chivying them
around. He was greatly influenced by the recent visit of a troop
of the Kings African Rifles and modeled himself on the way the
Sergeant ordered the Askari about. He would attempt to order
about other African, who came to the department with
complaints, although this didn't always come off dependent on
which tribe he was dealing with.

The state of the Messengers uniforms was deplorable, their tunics
and shorts were thread bare and so badly torn that attempts to
clip them together, using the office stapling machine had totally
failed. I had noticed when taking over the stores that there were
plenty of uniforms in stock and, it seemed to me that a new issue
was long overdue. Panjawani said this would not be a good idea
but, apart from the need to amend the Stores Ledger and order
new stock, he offered no specific reason for his objections.
Compared with the turn-out of the Messengers employed at the
Provincial Headquarters the appearance of my own staff was
deplorable and I could see no reason why a new issue should not
be made forthwith. The Messengers received their new clothing
with obvious delight, made all the greater because they were
aware that Panjawani disapproved of the whole operation.
Maloda quickly got word to the Sweepers at the Transit Centre
whose clothing was if anything worse than that of the Messengers.
For this reason there seemed to be no point in requesting that
existing uniforms be returned to store. Panjawani went through
the whole operation without further comment other than shaking
his head at what he obviously considered to be the folly of an inexperienced newly appointed officer. It turned out that he was
absolutely right and I was completely wrong.

The next morning the Messengers and Sweepers, with the

exception of Maloda, appeared wearing the remnants of their old uniforms. I asked Aron to find out why they were not wearing their new issue, but it took him some time to get any kind of answer and eventually he reported that they claimed to have lost them.

'What, all of them?

'So they say, Sir – but I think they have probably sold them.'

'Where on earth could they sell them in a place like this?'

After some thought Aron replied, 'Probably to the Arab or Somali traders in the market or even one of the local tailors'. As there are no Government markings on them he thought that they might also have been sold in the commercial or private sectors. He also considered that wherever they had sold them for they would only get about a quarter of their value if that.

Panjawani remained silent throughout this exchange but could scarcely hide his smug satisfaction at the way things had turned out.

'Aron, I want all the Messengers and Sweepers on the veranda in an hours time wearing their new uniforms. Will you make this clear to them?'

'Certainly Sir' and off he went.

They duly assembled with Maloda chivying them into some sort of line. With the exception of Maloda not one of them had paraded in his new uniform and all were looking fairly shifty as though expecting trouble.

'Aron, ask them why they are not wearing the new uniforms they were given yesterday.'

Aron then went down the line asking each one in turn the responses varying between 'I don't know' or 'Some one stole them' or 'I think I have lost them' or just silence.

'Aron, will you explain to them that the uniforms are not mine, nor are they Pajawani's, they are the property of the Government.   Uniforms are issued to them because the Government requires that they should be properly dressed when they are employed on Government duties.'

After Aron had translated this I asked him to get them to say whether they understood what I was saying and this eventually produced a reluctant 'Yes'. Through Aron I then informed them that anyone who takes the property of Government and loses it, or sells it, or destroys it, commits an offence and must expect to be punished. I also asked him to ask them if they understood what I was saying.

Aron again pressed them into a reluctant acknowledgment but no one had anything to say. At this point the atmosphere was tangible as it must have occurred to them that one outcome might be their summary dismissal. It was also clear that Panjawani, Aron and Jonathan, were watching events very closely and had an obvious interest in how I was going to deal with this. For myself I couldn't believe that they could have behaved so stupidly and I had the feeling that there must be something going on here which I failed to understand. However, there seemed to be little point in allowing the situation to continue unresolved so, again through Aron, I told them that the reasons the had given me were totally unacceptable and that I had concluded that they had behaved stupidly and dishonestly and that they deserve to be dismissed. They were obviously very concerned about this possibility and it was apparent that the concept of losing their jobs had never occurred to them. After a certain amount of muttering in Chigogo they asked Aron to explain that they were sorry but, as I was a new Bwana, they were not sure if I would be 'kali' (fierce) or not. I suppose what they were really saying was that because I was new they were not certain how much they might get away with. I then told them that that I had decided to treat them like Askari pointing out that if a soldier lost his equipment the cost of such a loss was immediately deducted from his pay. In this case I would ask Mr. Panjawani to check up on the costs of their uniforms and to make the necessary deductions from all their wages starting at the end of the month. I also explained that I would immediately authorise an issue of new uniforms which henceforth would be kept in the Department and which they would wear when they came on duty and leave behind when work finished at the end of each day. I also warned them that the loss of any item of uniform would result in summary dismissal. Their reaction was an animated discussion in Chigogo and Swahili, which Aron promptly cut short and dismissed them.

My office was pleasant enough with standard government office
furniture in the form of a desk, a glass fronted bookcase
containing a complete set of the Laws of Tanganyika including the
Laws Of Evidence and the Criminal Procedure Code. In addition
to chairs and an overhead electric fan there were two large
windows, one overlooking the Boma at the front and one at the
side overlooking the Magistrates Court; these were always kept
tightly shut, notwithstanding the heat, for reasons I was yet to
discover. The desk had the usual In and Out trays and the
'Kengele' – a highly polished brass bell operated by striking a
knob on its top. The code for this was very simple, I ring for
Pajawani, 2 for Aron, 3 for Jonathan and 4 for a Messenger;
answered without fail by Maloda. The only interior decoration in
the office was the standard Government issue of the Map of
Tanganyika which provided the basis for planning safaris
throughout the Central Province. So far as my duties and
responsibilities were concerned there was no formal job
description and I would have to rely on the explanations I was
given by my predecessor at the time of the hand over. Bearing in
mind his final advice 'not to worry, everything is in the files'.
Fortunately the Department operated a system of written Reports
which were submitted to Headquarters every three months
describing the activities of each of the Provincial Labour Offices
under a prescribed set of headings. I found these quite helpful
since they contained a summary of the Departments operations
reaching back over a number of years including precedents on a
wide range of issues which provided some guidance in dealing
with current problems.

On the basis of these reports it was evident that I was responsible
for the administration and implementation of Government's
labour and employment policies throughout the Province –
primarily securing compliance with and enforcement of the
Employment Ordinance and its Regulations and the Factories Act
with special emphasis on safety, health and welfare. On a
practical day to day basis, this meant dealing with issues such as
recruitment and migration to employment, complaints and
disputes between employers and workers, child labour and terms
and conditions of employment. So far as enforcement was

concerned, where necessary cases would have to be prosecuted in the District Court but from what I could see in the Reports this was much discussed but seldom attempted. There was also a requirement for me to liaise with the Provincial Commissioner on matters of security or political significance as a member of the Provincial Security Committee. On the face of it this looked like a pretty formidable challenge but, as with most things, there would be precedents relating to most issues particularly the application of legislation. What was going to be crucial in the short term was that I should acquire a sound working knowledge of the laws and equally important fluency in Kiswahili. So far as labour administration was concerned, the reports of my predecessors would help and Aron had day to day experience of dealing with complaints and settling minor disputes. So far as technical aspects of factories inspections were concerned, I could see no special difficulty here. In my former military service I had spent some years as the Officer in Charge of a Heavy Anti Aircraft Workshop whilst serving in the Royal Electrical and Mechanical Engineers. Perhaps the most worrying aspect of all this was the scale of operations since the Central Province covered an area the size of Wales. Inspecting all the employing concerns and factory premises scattered throughout the Province would certainly call for a comprehensive and time consuming programme of safaris given the distances involved. My predecessor, like many other Labour Officers, had chosen to use his own private car to undertake such safaris claiming reimbursement from Government at prescribed mileage rates. However, since I didn't possess a car, I had been assured that the Department would provide me with a vehicle and driver but these had yet to appear.

In the event what appeared to be a formidable travel programme turned out to be less demanding than the map of the Territory seemed to suggest. A close look at the map showing the Central Province revealed hundreds of square miles of empty bush occupied fairly sparsely by the Wagogo tribe. They were surviving on traditional subsistence agriculture barely achieving self-sufficiency with little or no agricultural surplus except in those rare years when rainfall was above average. Industrial undertakings, such as they were, were confined to Dodoma Township. These were mainly workshops operated by Government establishments such as the Public Works Department, the East African Railways, the Water Development Department and the Geological Surveys. In addition there were Rice and Oil Mills owned and operated by local Asian businessmen, as were building contractors and wood working factories. Other employers included Missions set up by the Church Missionary Society, American Christian Missions and Italian Catholics which, in addition to their religious, clinical and educational activities operated mechanised farms with associated workshops; the Italians had also managed to establish a vineyard producing a wine labeled 'Dodoma Red'. Similar employing concerns were repeated on a smaller scale in the other Townships such as Manyoni, Itigi, Singida, Kondoa, Mpapwa and Gulwe. In some cases Townships gave an exaggerated impression of their real status, they were little more than Stations on the Central Railway line where water and fuel were available for servicing trains and around which trading posts had been established providing markets for local produce, cattle and hides and skins. All of these were reached by unmettaled roads, dusty and badly corrugated, which in the rainy season were often disrupted and sometimes closed as bridges and culverts were washed away by flash floods sweeping across Ugogo.

FIRST INSPECTION

Where to start had to be decided but concentration on a programme of action was not easily achieved since the thoughts uppermost in my mind were with my son Peter, still in hospital in Dar es Salaam and news about his progress was not easy to come by. So, as a first step I decided to divide my working day into dealing with routine office matters, complaints, and studying the laws, in the mornings with inspections in the afternoons. Somewhere into the programme had to be fitted study of Kiswahili but, in the event, this had to be done in the evenings at home. Looking through the files I noticed that there was a stone quarry just on the edge of town along the railway line but on which there was no inspection report. Since this was less than two miles away from the office I decided to visit it taking Aron with me and Maloda who claimed to have been there before. Finding it under Maloda's guidance was no problem but I was surprised to find that it was something less than a quarry in the sense there was no deep excavation from which minerals were being extracted. Instead we came upon a pile of rocks and huge boulders sticking up out of the bush round the bottom of which some 30 or 40 elderly Africans were squat on the ground using hand hammers to break up boulders into small pieces suitable for ballast on the railway line.

The person in charge was a young Asian youth about 14 or 15 years old who occupied a small store made of mud and wattle with a thatched roof. At first he was really frightened, mistaking Aron's uniform as that of a policeman. After some reassurance he explained that this was his fathers business and that he had a sub-contract to supply ballast to the Railway Superintendent. The system of working couldn't have been simpler, the workers were paid on a task basis the task being to fill a Karai (a large metal basin) with small pieces of rock of a suitable size for ballast. A register was kept of all the workers showing payments made at

the end of each day and the workers thumb prints were recorded
against each payment. All the workers, who seemed to be grey
haired much wrinkled old men, responded to Aron's enquiry's to
the effect that they were paid on a regular basis but all
complained that the wages were too low. I found the whole
business pretty disturbing, every one was working in the hot sun
without shade, there was no evidence of food or even drinking
water and it was obvious that there were no sanitary
arrangements. I felt that I ought to make some sensible comment
so, turning to Aron I asked

'About how much would these chaps earn on a normal day?'

Aron looked at me in some amazement and replied, 'Well Sir,
these chaps are all women'.

There seemed to be no answer to that so we made our way back
to the Department.

On the way back I discussed my concerns about the absence of
shade, drinking water sanitary facilities first aid equipment etc.
with Aron. He patiently explained that these people were all
casual labour, engaged without any formal contract or hours of
work and in these circumstances the usual care and welfare
regulations did not apply. He also explained that some Asian
employers engaged in this form of sub-contract work were well
aware of this and were careful not to offer permanent
employment to anyone for this reason. I commented that without
these workers the business would cease to operate and it was
obvious that the work was hot, dusty and sometimes dangerous.
Accidents could easily happen when lifting heavy rocks and the
constant hammering could doubtless result in damaged fingers
and that no first aid equipment was available. Aron's reactions
to this were fairly negative pointing out that we had no legal
authority in cases like this. He went on to say that if Samji, the
Contractor, turned out to be like some other Asian employers he
could mention, he would not accept any direction from us that
was not backed up by law. Back at the office I mentioned this
situation to Panjawani who said he knew Samji and was inclined
to agree with Aron's assessment, pointing out that without any
power under the law it would be impossible to get a satisfactory
response from Samji.

The situation out at the quarry still troubled me so I called a meeting with Aron and Panjawani and suggested that whilst I agreed that we had no legal powers to intervene, surely no sensible employer would want to get on the wrong side of the Department unnecessarily. I proposed as a first step that I call Mr. Samj into the office to discuss the outcome of our visit to the quarry and suggest to him that he should provide some improvements in line with our findings. I also accepted Aron's advice that even if Samji agreed to provide sanitary arrangements the workers would not use them so we should drop this issue. They both responded in the same way saying that without legal powers we would be wasting our time with someone like Samji. I pointed out that whilst we may not have the power of labour legislation behind us this did not mean that we could have no influence. For example, if Samji refused to make any modest improvements, we could let him know that we would have no alternative but to alert the District Superintendent of Railways that we consider the conditions at the quarry to be really unsatisfactory. We could suggest that he might wish to take this into account before issuing further contracts for ballast. Aron quickly saw the point and a huge grin spread over his face as he said he would call Samji in for a meeting as soon as he could contact him.

In the event Samji turned out to be just as recalcitrant as Aron and Panjawani had predicted. He argued that at the wages he was paying the workers he was scarcely breaking even and any additional costs would turn a marginal business into a failure. He went on to say that he had never had any problems with Labour Officers in the past and could see no reason why welfare issues should now be raised - particularly as he was not breaking any laws.

'Mr Samji, I am not accusing you of breaking the law which I agree does not cover the situation at the quarry.'

'Right then what is all the fuss about?'

'The fuss, as you describe it, is about the need to provide a few simple, inexpensive improvements for the benefit of your employees.'

'Why should I when I have never had to do this before.'

'Well, lets get these costs into some sort of perspective. So far as water is concerned, all that is necessary is that when you take your son out to the quarry each morning you take two debbies of water and these could be brought back empty each evening. I wouldn't regard that as expensive.'

'Well, they would still need a cup to drink from.'

'Alright, and a cup. You can get a first aid kit from Remtullahs duka so that should not be a problem.'

'I wouldn't buy anything from Remtullah on principle.'

'Lets talk about the shelter, this needs to be no more than a thatched roof supported on poles with open sides; any fundi could make this from local materials at very modest costs, don't you agree.'

'It would still cost something and would have to be maintained.'

'So far as costs are concerned you must be aware, as a business man, that reasonable costs on care and welfare items are tax deductable. I would be happy to speak to the Revenue Officer about this if you think it would help.'

Mention of tax and the Revenue Office caused an immediate change in Samji's attitude and it occurred to me that he may not be paying tax on his quarry earnings.

'I will deal with my own tax affairs without any outside interference.'

'Well, Mr. Samji I think we both understand each other and I suggest that you now give some thought to what has been said and what action you should take. I think it would be a pity if our relationship were to get off to a poor start because of lack of cooperation.'

'I am not breaking any law and I am just as good an employer as many others round here.'

'Mr. Samji, am I right in thinking that you own Samji's Saw Mill which is registered with my Department as a factory?'

'I am joint owner with my brother.'

'In that case I think we will be seeing something of each other in my capacity of Factory Inspector and on that occasion you may wish to keep in mind that I shall be exercising full legal powers under the Factories Act. Let me know what you decide about the quarry.'

After he had left the office Panjawani said 'He is a hard case but that business about the Revenue Officer has got him worried so he will probably agree'.

I asked Aron to keep an eye on this and a week later he reported that there was now water and a first aid kit at the quarry but the shelter was just poles with a large canvas cover over the top.

PART 3

MIGRANT LABOUR AND
ATTESTATIONS

Because of the uncertain rain patterns in the Central Province and consequent poor harvests, the Wagogo tribe were sometimes obliged to seek employment outside the Province. Employment opportunities were often available for unskilled labour on sisal estates in the Eastern Province and on mixed farms in the Northern Province particularly during the pyrethrum, sugar and coffee harvest. It was for this reason that the Department operated the two Labour Transit Centres in Dodoma and at Itigi both on the Central Railway line. Migration to employment offered a reasonable alternative to surviving on famine relief, particularly in areas where the long and short rains had failed in the same year. Employers in the Sisal Industry and agricultural employers in the Northern Province engaged licensed Recruiters to supply labour on Attested Contracts which were prescribed under labour legislation and administered by the Labour Department. The terms and conditions under which such migrant labour was employed conformed with the provisions of an International Labour Convention which had been ratified by the United Kingdom. The primary purpose of the Convention was to ensure that all such migrant labour was recruited on a strictly voluntary basis. Also that the terms of the contract, i.e. the wages to be paid, rations and housing to be provided and other care and welfare facilities the workers would be entitled to, were clearly defined and understood by the workers concerned at the point of recruitment. Generally speaking such migrant labour was undertaken by adult, fit, males but in the case of long term contracts, or where the drought was particularly severe, provision was made for workers to be accompanied by their families.

The demand for migrant workers was fairly constant dependent on the season but the response of the Wagogo invariably depended on the success or otherwise of the last harvest. Since the Central Province was regarded as a source of unskilled labour by major employing concerns outside the Province the Department played a crucial role in monitoring the activities of licensed Recruiters and ensuring that the Transit Centres provided adequate shelter and welfare facilities for workers in transit. Recruiters were obliged by law to have all migrant workers formally attested by a Labour Officer who would only sign contracts when satisfied that the workers concerned were those listed on the contract and that each worker understood and accepted the terms and conditions and, in particular, the duration of the contract. The employers' responsibilities for transport costs and repatriation to the point of recruitment at the successful completion of the contract were also clearly defined. The whole migrant labour process produced a conflicting set of interests. The licensed Recruiter, acting on behalf of the employer, has a vested interest in persuading workers to accept contract labour – he was paid on a per capita basis and would sometimes offer unspecified inducements to achieve his purpose. The Labour Officer had a duty to safeguard the interests of the workers, in particular to ensure that all attested labour was voluntary and that each worker understood all the provisions of the contract before signing it. Since most workers could neither read nor write and the contracts were printed in English affixing individual finger prints against the appropriate name on the contract signified consent.

The Attestation Forms were drafted to conform with an International Labour Organisation Convention on Migration to Employment which in turn was drafted by a Committee of Experts working in one of the richest city's in the world. Such Committees were made up of representatives of Governments, Employers Organisations, and Trade Unions where direct experience of working conditions in a third world plantation would be at a premium. So, it would not be surprising if what was desirable was sometimes substituted for what was practical in the interests of securing tri-partite agreement. During the attestation

process some workers would change their minds and withdraw so
the Recruiter would complain that official interference was
limiting the success of the recruitment process. Consequently,
Employers Associations would then complain to the Labour
Advisory Board claiming that Labour Officers were too rigid in
carrying out attestations. Paradoxically, they would also
complain that Labour Officers were remiss in explaining the
duration of the contract period with the result that there was an
unacceptable level of desertions. It was certainly the case that the
Wagogo had an unenviable reputation for walking back home
long before the completion of their 12 months or in some cases 2
year contracts. Such desertions were often influenced by word
getting to them that good rains had fallen in their tribal area and
distance never seemed to be a problem. Cynics would say that the
only Wagogo who ever completed a two year contract were those
recruited to work in Zanzibar since none of them had managed to
walk across the Zanzibar Channel. An additional factor in the
migrant labour issue was the attitude of the local District Officers
who disliked labour migrations' negative impact on the collection
of 'Kodi', a form of hut tax, the collection of which was one of
their major responsibilities.

Migrant labour problems featured prominently in the Reports of
my predecessors and it was clear that I would need to keep a very
careful eye on the whole attestation process. Because of my as yet
limited Swahili, I was very dependent on Aron the Labour
Inspector, and, because of his knowledge of Chigogo, Maloda. A
typical attestation would run along the following lines.
     Panjawani would come into my office with a batch of
Attestation Contracts and inform me that a Recruiter had arrived
with some workers for attestation.
     'Good, call Aron and get him to line them up facing the
verandah.'
     The Recruiter would then appear, in this case a Mr.Firenzi
who normally recruited for the sisal industry. He was about 45 to
50 years of age and claimed to be a Seychellois but from his
appearance seemed to be part Arab part Swahili. However, he
spoke fluent English but like most Recruiters he gave the

impression of being nervous and uncertain with a slightly worrying disposition which seemed to go with the job.

'Hello Mr. Ferenzi, what do you have for us today?'

'Good afternoon Sir, I have a batch of recruits for a sisal estate in Morogoro, there are 11 outside and 2 more will be here shortly. Mr. Panjawani has the forms.'

'Fine, where have they come from?'

'Most of them from Manyoni district but 4 from Dodoma.'

'Good, do they know what its all about?'

'Oh yes I have been through the form in detail and you will find that they have a pretty good understanding as to where they are going. They will stay at the Transit Centre tonight and get the mixed goods train to Morogoro in the morning.'

'Fine, well lets have a look at them.'

Outside facing the verandah Aron had them lined up and Maloda was chivying them about trying to get them in line whilst Aron was checking their names against the attestation forms; there were still 2 men missing.

Judging from their appearance they all seemed to be Wagogo but Maloda pointed out that 2 of them were Wapogoro which raised the possibility that they were only interested in a free train journey back to their tribal district. All were wearing a shuka or blanket over their shoulders and, apart from a panga or a throwing stick, they had no other possessions. They clearly regarded me with some suspicion and had doubtless been warned by Firenzi not to say anything.

Anyway, this was an opportunity for me to try out some of my newly acquired swahili so I started with – 'Jambo, u hali gani – hello, how are you? This was received in complete silence although one or two smiled – probably at my strange pronunciation.

Aron then spoke to them rather sharply saying 'Sema Jambo' – say hello, at which they all looked nervously at the Recruiter and eventually muttered 'Jambo Bwana'. So I continued, 'Una Kwenda ku fanya kazi wapi?' Again this evoked no response until Aron said 'Tell the Bwana where you are going to work'. Again complete silence until Aron repeated the question addressing one of the younger men who then replied 'Sijui – I don't know'.

So much for Ferenzi's assurance that he had explained the terms of the contract.
'Alright Aron, we will have to go through the whole contract item by item.'

Under these arrangements it was explained that :-
They were going to work on a sisal estate near Morogoro which was very far and they would travel by train.
They would be paid Shgs 75 for each 30 day ticket they completed.
They would be given a blanket and a cooking pot which they would keep.
They would be fed posho (maize meal) every day and red palm oil, tea, fruit, sugar, salt and meat three times a week.
They would be given a room to sleep in and water for drinking and washing and 'kuni' (firewood) for cooking.
If they became sick they would be given 'dawa' (medicine) to make them better.
They would be returned to Dodoma at the completion of their 12months contract. It was also explained that if they agreed to take this kind of employment they must sign a 'Karatasi' – a paper – by putting their thumb print indicating their agreement. Finally it was explained that if they did not want to go they need not sign and were free to return home. It took some time to get this information across and much of it had to be repeated. At the end of this process I took the opportunity to try out my swahili again by asking them where were they going to and finally got the reply 'mbali sana' – a very long way; no one could remember Morogoro. When asked what they would do there they replied 'to do some work' and when asked about their rations they were content with the expression 'tumepata chackula' – we will get food. They all seemed to understand that they would get Sgs. 75 per ticket but one or two of them had no idea what a ticket was. When asked if they wished to ask any questions there was complete silence so Aron asked if they all agreed to go to work and on this basis their names were checked on the Attestation Contracts. Maloda with much performing then got them to put their thumbprints on the form against each name. Since the two additional recruits had not appeared their names were struck off

and I signed the Attestation much to Ferenzi's relief. It was not unusual during this process for one or two workers to withdraw and sometimes I found it necessary to refuse to accept people on grounds of age, obvious mental deficiency, partial blindness, tropical ulcers etc.

After an attestation I made a point of visiting the Transit Centre later in the day to do a final check, sometimes with surprising results. That is to find that some of the original volunteers had been replaced by others who had not been attested, or other recruits who were obviously under age or physically unsuitable. Understandably employers saw desertion as a major and

Attesting Migrant Workers

expensive hazard in recruiting migrant labour and their complaints on this issue were frequent and sometimes intemperate. On one occasion a South African employer who had a mixed farm near Mpapwa came in to the Department to complain over his desertion problems. He had quite obviously been drinking and offered his own unique solution to the problem. It was generally accepted that women were far better workers than men, more productive and likely to cause less trouble in the labour lines. His proposition was that he should pay the 'bride price' for about a dozen Wagogo women instead of recruiting fees and thus secure a permanent and stable labour force. Whilst I had to agree that such an arrangement would not contravene any labour legislation I suggested, however, that, as a first step, he might wish to discuss the concept with his wife; knowing her I could see little prospect of such an idea ever getting off the ground. The whole labour migration business, no matter how carefully administered, always left me with an uneasy feeling of disquiet, particularly when seen from the viewpoint of the recruit. Most of the men who were persuaded to accept long term employment offered by Recruiters were ordinary tribesmen whose lifestyles were molded within the tribal environment. Through no fault of their own they were uneducated and illiterate but by no means unintelligent. On the contrary, they had come to terms with living and surviving in the challenging, tropical environment of the semi desert conditions of the Central Province where people like me, left to my own devices, would probably starve. They had built their own houses, cultivated their own shambas using traditional methods and would normally raise crops of maize, millet, cassava and vegetables. Given reasonable rain they could grow sufficient to sustain themselves and their families and retain seed for next years planting. In a good year they might grow a cash crop and a surplus of maize to allow them to brew beer as well as sell hides and skins, charcoal, honey, beeswax, and gum-Arabic. With astute bartering they could acquire and breed cattle and small stock such as goats, sheep, and chickens and also find the bride price for additional wives or wives for their sons. Within the limits of the Chiefs authority they enjoyed a level of independence earned through self-reliance which they cherished. They were their own men with their own dignity, entitled to speak at 'barazas' – tribal gatherings – and they enjoyed respect within their own community.

All this was put at risk when, as sometimes happened, the rains failed catastrophically and resort to paid employment was seen as the only option; particularly if part of their earnings could be sent back to sustain their families. Consequently, few migrant workers could be induced to stay on beyond the contract period and, as mentioned earlier, the temptation to break their contracts often proved difficult to resist. Against this background, agricultural employers were obliged to widen the search for recruited labour even beyond the Territorial borders. However, experience showed that workers recruited from as far away as Ruanda-Urundi produced nothing but trouble in the Transit Centres and the labour lines on estates. Following an investigation into this it turned out that the Belgian authorities were giving people convicted in the courts the option of a prison sentence or serving on attested contracts. What I always found disquieting about the migrant labour business was the fact that historically Ugogo was an area through which the old slave trade used to pass. Slaves were mainly taken from the Western and the Lake Provinces where people had better food choices and were physically fitter that the Wagogo but the Gogo Chiefs were notorious for charging exorbitant rates of 'Hongo' i.e. gifts and guns which they demanded for allowing slavers safe passage through their Chiefdoms on the way to and from the coast. Moving workers even with all the safeguards of the Attested Contracts system still left me with a slight feeling of people being moved against their will.. I often felt that they would be better off at home, even though they may be on famine relief for a while.

ENCOUNTER WITH THE MAGISTRATE

The Departmental Office was located alongside the District Court and in the open space between the two buildings the Resident magistrate would normally park his car. It was in this space that people waiting to attend the court would sit until their case was called. The Magistrate, named Wyllie, a seriously overweight former Administrative Officer, was well known for his short temper and his relations with Africans something less than a model of racial tolerance. He was a tall, balding, pear shaped, perspiring and noisy individual, with the kind of knock knees that might have looked better had he worn slacks as opposed to a huge pair of shorts. It seemed to give him pleasure to drive up to the parking space as fast as possible slamming on the brakes at the last moment. People waiting would scatter in fear of their lives and the sliding car would throw up a huge cloud of dust which took ages to settle. It was for this reason that the windows on both sides of my office were kept permanently closed notwithstanding the heat and reliance had to be placed on the ceiling fan to keep the place cool.

It was Wyllie who, on our first being introduced, lectured me to the effect that I would have to realise that no one liked or trusted Labour Officers and that this was something I would have to get used to. It was clear from the outset that, despite the fact that we were both former army officers, Wyllie for some reason retaining his army rank, we were unlikely to become comrades. In response to my suggestion that he might take a more measured approach when parking his car he also pointed out that dust was a fact of life in Africa and that this was something else I would have to get used to. During Court sessions he could be heard shouting at the accused, the witnesses, the prosecutor and sometimes the defending council and I was soon to learn that despite all the bombast he was not particularly competent in his magisterial duties – the High Court would from time to time throw out his judgements much to his fury. This was worrying since my duties would require me to conduct prosecutions in respect of contravention's of the Employment Ordinance and the Factories Act. Experience was to show that by shouting at witnesses and constantly interrupting the prosecution process, the outcome of court proceedings could seldom be predicted. Convictions seemed to depend more on the Magistrate's idiosyncratic interpretation of the law rather than the evidence before the Court and sentencing was even less predictable.

Our relationship was not much improved when the Department received a complaint over unpaid wages by Wyllie's long suffering cook who had surprisingly managed to stay in post for over three years. This was remarkable since the Magistrate had a reputation for aggressively treating his servants and complaints about improper dismissal from house-boys, dhobis and shamba-boys had almost become a commonplace. Wyllie's elderly cook was known to be very competent and seemingly able to tolerate erratic behaviour such as being called out of bed at 2 or 3 in the morning so as to cook bacon and eggs for guests brought back from drinking sessions at the Club. The cook was an Nyamwezi who came from the Western Province and for family reasons wished to return home to his tribal district. In accordance with his contract he had given one months notice of his intention to leave which Wyllie in a fit of temper refused to accept. The cook came to the Department for advice and Aron very properly advised him that he was entitled to leave and suggested that he gave notice in writing. Since the cook could neither read nor write Aron drafted a suitable letter which the Magistrate promptly tore up.

At the end of the month the cook packed up his belongings, vacated his quarters and asked for his wages which were refused. After a great deal of shouting and threatening Wyllie told his cook that he could have two weeks leave and half his months pay, the balance to be paid when he returned to duty. Since the cook was now determined to leave he made a formal complaint over failure to pay wages to the Department and Aron came in to ask me how he should proceed. I told him that the Magistrate should be treated just like any other employer in similar circumstances and that he should make out the standard Complaint Form setting out the cook's allegations and seeking the employer's response.

I asked Aron to let me see the Form before it issued and when this appeared on my desk it was evident that it had been correctly completed and there seemed to be no reason why I should not allow it to be issued. However, a situation such as this was bound to attract attention, particularly amongst the African and Asian communities some of whom would take some pleasure at the Magistrate being obliged to account for his behaviour. With this in mind I decided as a first step to see Wyllie in the hope that the matter could be settled without resort to the formal procedure. I chose a time when the Court was not in session and found the Magistrate in his office.

'Hello, could I see you for a moment?'

'You don't have an appointment – I hope this is not something trivial.'

'Its not something trivial to me, its what I'm paid to do.'

'I see, well, lets get on with it.'

'I have had a formal complaint from your cook who claims he wishes to terminate his contract, has given due notice and now claims the wages which are now due.'

Wyllie then stood up shouting 'I don't need you to interfering in my domestic affairs. What I do with my servants is my private business and in any case the matter has already been resolved – I have decided to give him 14 days leave and half pay.'

'This may be a convenient arrangement for you but he doesn't accept it – he intends to leave your employment and is claiming the wages to which he says he is entitled to.'

'Don't you dare come into my office trying to tell me what the law is. I have been administering the law years before you set foot in Africa.'

'I am not here to tell you the law, we both know that in a situation like this the legal position is quite clear, so I was simply hoping that between us we could agree on a solution to this claim.'

'I don't need to agree anything with you so get back to your office and stop fooling about in matters you don't understand – do I make myself clear?'

'Stopping fooling about, as you describe it, is not an option for me unless these wages are paid my continued involvement is beyond question, even to the point of legal action if this becomes the last resort.'

'What on earth do you mean – don't you know that you are dealing with a Magistrate?'

'I'm well aware of that but so far as I am concerned you are also an employer and if we can't reach a sensible solution, I am obliged to follow the procedure for recovering wages when due just as I would with any other employer.'

'I am not prepared to listen to this nonsense in my own Chambers and I order you to leave my office immediately.'

'If that's the way you feel I'm off. But I hope you will give this further thought and reach a satisfactory solution. As you are probably aware, there are a number of cooks registered as seeking employment at my Department.' By now Wyllie seemed to be heading for some kind of heart attack so I promptly withdrew.

Back at the office it was obvious that the staff had been able to hear much of the Magistrates shouting although, because I am normally quietly spoken, it was unlikely that they would have heard my contribution. Panjawani who was in constant fear of the Magistrate was quite pale and Aron too was looking pretty worried. Maloda on the other hand was quite excited but how much of what was happening he really understood was a matter for speculation. I explained that I had tried to get a settlement with the Magistrate without success because he claims to have sorted it out. I asked Aron to call the cook in so that I could be satisfied that he really did want to terminate his employment and to review his pay claim. Having been assured on both these points I told Aron to send a messenger to the Court to deliver the Complaint Form making sure that it was addressed personally to the Magistrate. In the meantime Wyllie drove away from the Court creating the usual cloud of dust and loudly sounding his horn.

The next morning Wyllie stormed into my office waving the Complaint Form and demanded to know why I had allowed it to be sent to him signed by a 'bloody African'. I explained that in this Department all Complaint Forms are routinely signed by the Labour Inspector who investigates complaints in the first instance. I went on to point out that in this case I had personally checked the contents of the Form and approved them. In absolute fury he shouted 'Is this all you have to say?'

'Well, one other thing, why not pay the chap his wages then we can all get back to more important issues?'

'This has gone far enough, I am going to have this nonsense stopped immediately.' He then strode off angrily in the direction of the Boma. Panjawani was aghast and looking terribly worried said 'Sir, he is going to make a lot of trouble for us'.

'Well, he may make a lot of noise but we have to remember that the law is on our side, if he does make trouble it may be for himself, what do you think Aron?'

Aron looked pretty tense but seemed to have a firmer grip on things and replied 'Well Sir, Panjawani is right he really is mad so we should watch out for trouble, he won't leave this alone. What are we going to do Sir?'

'Aron, when an employer refuses to pay wages and we are convinced it is right to claim what do we normally do?'

Looking slightly bemused Aron replied 'We prosecute, Sir, but this is the District Magistrate, how can we prosecute him in his own Court?'

'Not even Wyllie can hear a case against himself in his own Court so we take him to the District Commissioner, who is also a Magistrate and probably a better one when it comes to a point of law.'

A few minutes later Panjawani answered a phone call from the Boma and said 'Sir, it's the P.Cs. office, the Provincial Commissioner wants to see you immediately'. A few seconds later the phone rang again and I got the message that my son Peter had been discharged from hospital and would be arriving in Dodoma on the afternoon flight from Dar es Salaam. I immediately sent Maloda off with a note to Wyn with the good news and couldn't have gone to a meeting in a better frame of mind. On entering the P.C's office I was still smiling and the P.C. looked at me fairly quizzically and asked if there was something funny going on that he was unaware of. 'I'm sorry Sir, but I was told two minutes ago

that my son Peter has been discharged from hospital in Dar es
Salaam and will be arriving here on the afternoon flight. This is
the best news I've had since I arrived in Africa'. 'That is good
news, sit down, I have called you over to sort out the problem you
seem to be having with the Resident Magistrate'.

Wyllie was sitting on a chair facing the P.C.'s desk so I
occupied the only other chair.

'Mr. Wyllie tells me that he is being unduly harassed by your
Department can you tell me what's going on?'

'Sir, I deny that I or any of my staff have harassed anyone let
alone the Resident Magistrate.'

'Wyllie interrupted by waving the Complaint Form an saying
'How do you explain this accusing me of failing to pay my
servants wages and signed by an African?'

'Quite simply, if you trouble to read the Form, and try to set
aside the fact that it is signed by an African, you will see that it
makes no accusations whatsoever. This is the standard form used
for dealing with complaints throughout my Department. It sets
out a complaint we have received from an employee and invites
the employer to respond. My Labour Inspector, who signed this
Form is simply doing the job for which he has been trained and is
paid by government to perform.'

The P.C. then asked to see the Form which he quickly read
then making the remark 'I don't see any harassment about that,
Mr. Wyllie is there something else we should be discussing?'

'Well Sir, it's the general attitude I object to, after all I am the
Resident Magistrate and I do not expect to be formally confronted
with alleged complaints by junior staff of a subordinate
Department.'

The P.C. looked over and said 'Glynn, do you have anything
to say about that?'

'Sir, its clear from the Form that none of my staff have alleged
anything all that is recorded is the complaint of Mr Wyllie's
employee.'

Wyllie then interrupted by saying 'So you think it is alright for
a junior member of your staff to come round to my Court and
serve me with one of these things?' To which I replied 'With
respect, before that form issued, I made a point of consulting you
and alerting you to the fact that I had received a complaint and

to let you have details. It was your view then that I was messing about in something I didn't understand and that you had sorted the problem out by offering your cook half the wages he was entitled to and granting him 14 days leave. It was only after I had verified that your cook would not accept your offer that the Form issued'. At this point the P.C. intervened by asking how I saw the matter being resolved.

'Well Sir, I hope that good sense will prevail and that the employees rights and entitlements be respected. He should get the wages now due and, since he has given proper notice, be allowed to go. The P.C. then asked what I saw as the next step to which I replied that if there could be no progress along the lines I had outlined resort to the court seemed to be the only option. The P.C. then asked if I could not see the absurdity of taking legal action against a sitting Magistrate. 'I couldn't agree more, particularly as in this case no attempt at conciliation had been made and the services of my Department have been rejected'.

'Conciliation along what lines?'

'Sir, in dealing with any other employer we would be finding out why the cook was so determined to leave and explore what might be done by way of incentives bearing in mind that he is good at his job and his employer wishes to retain him. Better pay, improved working hours, regular leave entitlement and, at the very least, agreement to continue working until a replacement could be found . In my view all these things are worth exploring but given Mr. Wyllie's attitude there seems to be no grounds for optimism in this case.'

'Alright Glynn, I think I understand your position in this we will see how things develop.'

As I was leaving the office the P.C. asked Wyllie to remain behind and I could only speculate about the direction further discussions would then take. Back at the department I set about confidence building, pointing out that absolutely no blame would be placed on the staff and that I accepted full responsibility for everything that had happened, so there was no need for anyone to worry. There was of course 'fitina', a swahili word for trouble, between me and the Resident Magistrate but this shouldn't affect the staff. I also told them that we should keep an eye on things as there might be some further developments following the

Provincial Commissioner's discussions with Mr. Wyllie. In the event things seemed to take a turn for the better when the cook called in to let Aron know that there had been a settlement and that he was going to collect his wages from the Court and was then ready to get the train home. On receiving this news there were sighs of relief all round.

In the meantime we were all at the airport, a sandy landing strip, to meet Peter's plane. Peter emerged from the Dakota looking anxiously around and waved in response to our shouting. He then came carefully down the steps and although he was looking pale, as was to be expected, he was obviously delighted to see us all. Now we had the whole family together again and we couldn't wait to get him home, show him the house, and hear all his news. Later, when discussing his operation he produced a sealed envelope which was addressed to the District Medical Officer, Dodoma. We promptly whisked him off to the local hospital where he was examined and told to rest quietly for about two weeks but otherwise all was well.

Back at the Department there had been a further development as Maloda reported that, on the Magistrates orders, the cook had been arrested and taken to the police headquarters in handcuffs. In response to my inquiries, the Asian Sub-Inspector at the police station explained that having paid him his wages, the Magistrate demanded to see the cook's 'Kodi', (a form of pole-tax receipt) and since this could not be produced on the spot, ordered his arrest for tax evasion. Fortunately, when the cook was allowed to unpack his gear at the police station the 'Kodi' was found and he was released. This turned out to be a final piece of nastiness on the part of the Magistrate, which didn't come off. Maloda was dispatched to contact the cook and warn him to get down to the station with all his belongings and stop there until he could board the train for Tabora.

I had by now settled in to a satisfactory routine at the Department, dividing my time between administration, dealing with complaints, recruitment matters and factory inspections in Dodoma Township. I was still finding time to study the laws in the afternoons and to review the safari reports of my predecessors. My Swahili was slowly improving with an increased vocabulary but I still had a long way to go to master Swahili grammar which was essential if I was to have any hope of passing the advanced level examination. The absence of a departmental vehicle was a serious limiting factor and, although I had been assured that a vehicle would be made available when I left Headquarters in Dar es Salaam, this had yet to materialise. The factory inspections I had carried out thus far had been something of an eye opener and I had serious problems trying to reconcile the actual working conditions and safety arrangements in local workshops with the stringent requirements of the Factories Act. Most of the machinery was ancient and much repaired whilst secure fencing of dangerous moving parts amounted to little more than flimsy plywood guards where these existed at all.

The prime-movers in most workshops were old combustion engines running on gas oil, the flywheels of which powered a series of shafts and pulleys with belt drives to individual machines. Because of the many moving parts, hazards abounded all over the place but the incidence of accidents was not recorded anywhere and in some cases, my first reaction was to close the place down. Previous inspection reports on most of these places contained warnings to the employers that there was a need for immediate improvements in safety standards. However, while there was abundant evidence of contraventions of the Factories Act, there was no record of any prosecutions taking place. It seemed to me that the absence of sanctions had produced a general indifference to the requirements of the factories legislation. Most such undertakings were Asian owned family businesses, in which the family lived in part of the premises and often made up a key part of the labour force supplemented by African casual labour. In some establishments there had been reports of child labour being employed and this would certainly merit special attention.

TRANSPORT AND ABDULLAH ARRIVE

Aron accompanied me on these inspections and I was able to get his reactions to the conditions we were finding in different employing concerns. With a view to getting some kind of perspective on employment conditions generally I asked him how things in Dodoma compared with those prevailing in other Provinces in which he had been stationed. After giving the matter some thought he offered the view that the situation in Dodoma wasn't really too bad and that I would find things were worse in the smaller townships such as Manyoni, Singida, Kondoa and Mpapwa. As I was writing my inspection report on the Barmal Rice and Oil Mill, Panjawani came in to my office to announce that the driver had arrived.

'The driver, whose driver?'

'Yours Sir, he has brought his truck down from Moshi and says that he has now been transferred to Dodoma.'

'Have we been warned about this?'

'No Sir.'

(the letter notifying me of this arrived 10 days later)

'This is good news, lets have a look at them.'

By the side of the office was parked a fairly battered Ford 1 Ton Utility truck, with a wooden safari body, painted the standard green of all Government vehicles. This was being closely inspected by Aron, Maloda and the other Messengers. On the verandah Panjawni introduced the driver, Abdullah, who gave me a very relaxed languid salute that would have earned him 7 days confined to barracks in my former Regiment.

'Hello Adullah, welcome to Dodoma, I hope you had a good journey' – his hand shake was if anything even more relaxed than his salute. It turned out that he understood a limited amount of English but he replied 'Thank you, sir, but it was a very long journey'. He was about 45 to 50 years old, fairly tall and somewhat portly round the middle, wearing a khaki tunic with well polished brass buttons and belt buckle, slacks and a red fez and shoes. My impression was that he was part Arab part Swahili and a Muslim, all of which turned out to be the case. Accordingly, I must now remember never to give or take things from him with my left hand and also make sure he has time for prayer even though this may entail stopping the truck when on safari.

'You must be ready for something to eat and will need somewhere to stay although until this is sorted out you are welcome to use the Transit Centre. Aron, our Labour Inspecter will take you into town and help to get settled and our Chief Clerk, Mr. Panjawani will let you have an advance of salary if you feel this would be helpful'. It turned out that he had brought his wife and two children with him together with his luggage and had already dropped them off in the African quarter of the town. The next morning due to Panjawani's influence, Abdullah was given a Government quarter close to the town into which he settled without problems. It soon became clear that he was a serious practicing Muslim whose life style conformed rigorously with the tenets of his faith. He prayed four times a day, had his own prayer mat, attended the Mosque as often as his duties permitted and was fastidious about his diet. It also became clear that he

Abdullah, Maloda and Messengers
Ready for a Safari

regarded the Wagogo as a pack of infidels and his regard for Christians, though slightly more polite, was little better; Panjawani, as a Hindu came somewhere in the middle. However he had 12 years experience as a Government driver and would doubtless prove to be an asset in extending the scope of the Departments operations.

The truck was another matter, even a superficial examination indicated that it had completed a very substantial mileage, the tyres had certainly seen some action and the smoke coming from the exhaust confirmed that it was an oil burner. Events were to show that I would have plenty of opportunities to discover its strengths and weaknesses in due course. In the short term it offered an immediate solution to the dust problem created by the Magistrate's car. By employing the same tactics as he did in parking the truck between my office and the Court I was able to create a dust cloud that enveloped the Court building. This, as anticipated, led to an immediate and loud complaint from Wyllie and I was able to remind him that in his own words 'dust is a fact of life in Africa which we must all get used to'. He didn't like this at all but finally he had to modify his approach to parking and I was at last able to keep my office windows open.

Of course this did little to improve the relationship between the Magistrate and myself which was of some concern to me because, sooner or later I was going to take legal proceedings against local employers for serious breaches of the Factories Act and contra-ventions under the Employment Ordinance. There seemed to be little doubt that an objective judgement based on the facts of the case may not be achieved given Wyllie's attitude to me personally and my Department in general. If I was going to make an impression on the indifferent attitude of local employers a successful prosecution of two or three major offenders was going to be essential. What was obviously needed was convictions and the imposition of a substantial fine and a time based Court Order requiring remedial action. The chances of achieving such an outcome, particularly if the accused sought legal representation by the only local Advocate, who was known to be on good terms with the Magistrate, seemed at the very least uncertain. Nothing could be worse than taking a high profile case which would be carefully observed by most employers in the Township, and having it thrown out as 'No Case To Answer' or, in the case of a conviction, the imposition of a derisory fine or simple warning. It seemed apparent to me that there was overwhelming evidence of contraventions of the laws and it would be reasonable to assume that on the facts, properly presented in court, convictions by any reasonable Magistrate would be inevitable. My former military experience as an Adjutant provided me with adequate grounding in the laws of evidence and I was confident of my abilities as a prosecutor. However, against this background, it was obvious that to have any hopes of success I must try to establish a better working relationship with the Resident Magistrate. At the same time it had to be recognised that there were no grounds for optimism here since there was a personality conflict between us; put quite simply there was nothing I admired about him and he had even less respect for me.

SUMMARY JUSTICE?

Notwithstanding the need for some improvements in our relationship the situation was made infinitely worse when Wyllie, red in face and perspiring more that usual, stuck his head through my open window and shouted 'Come outside and see Summary Justice in action'. He reminded me of a school bully who had just done something of which he should be ashamed and was looking for moral support. Why he should be turning to me of all people remained a mystery. As I looked out of the window I could see a crowd of about 50 Wagogo had gathered in front of the Court building and three police Askari were trying to create an open space in the centre of the crowd. I met Aron and Maloda standing on the verandah watching developments as a Sergeant from the Prison Service arrived on a bicycle and reported to the Court office. Aron explained that a case of theft had just been concluded and the Magistrate had sentenced the offender to ten strokes of the cane. A public flogging was a very unusual sight indeed, but it was not something I wished to witness, Wyllie's invitation notwithstanding. However, as I turned to go back to my office the crowd started shouting in terms which suggested anger and derision. The focus of their anger was the Magistrate who had just emerged from the Court accompanied by the Court Clerk and two police Askari. Behind them was another Askari leading a small African boy, aged about 9 or 10, by his shoulders followed by the Prison Sergeant carrying a three foot long bamboo cane. Following them was a man and a woman, presumably the boy's parents, the later in tears supported by her husband and both greatly distressed.

I couldn't believe that such a small boy could be subjected to a public flogging, or a flogging of any kind, and I asked Aron of what crime had he been convicted. It turned out that the boy had been playing in the European quarter of the town when he came across a small child's tricycle abandoned at the side of the road near to a European residence; presumably forgotten by children who had returned home. Since there was no one about the boy had ridden the tricycle up and down the road but made no attempt to take it away. He was then caught by a patrolling police Askari who promptly arrested him taking the boy and the tricycle to the police station to be charged. Although the boy was of general good character and had no record of trouble he was charged with theft and appeared in court. The people outside the Court were obviously aware of this and news had spread quickly hence the size of the crowd and its resentment at the outcome. Regrettably, I was not aware of the details of the case as the punishment was administered. The boy was laid on the ground in front of the Court building, his trousers were removed and a handkerchief sized piece of dirty cloth was placed on his buttocks. Two Askari pinned the boy to the ground by his shoulders and ankles and the Prison Sergeant then reported to the Magistrate that he was ready and was given the order to proceed. The Sergeant then raised the cane high above his head and brought it down with full force on the boy's buttocks and reported 'Stroke One'. The Sergeant was experienced in administering punishment to hardened, adult, prisoners and was using the same force he would in Prison notwithstanding the age of the boy. The boy's scream of pain and shock evoked loud cries of anger from the crowd as the beating continued with strokes at three second intervals. I couldn't believe what I was seeing and my anger, indignation and embarrassment increased till at the third stroke I could stand it no longer and called to the Sergeant 'kidogo, kidogo, ametoto tu' – a little a little he is only a child'. This was the best Swahili I could manage and although inadequate the sergeant looked at me and seeing my anger, quickly finished strokes with very light taps; but of course the damage had been done. The boy's father was then allowed to pick up the boy, whose buttocks were bleeding and was in a semi-conscious state of shock, and carry him away accompanied by his distraught mother.

The crowd remained, various people shouting complaints and things began to look very unsettled. The Magistrate escorted by two Askari quickly re-entered the Court and the doors were closed, but it took some time for the crowd to disperse. Shortly afterwards I received a call from the Court Clerk requesting that I report to the Court immediately. On entering his office it was obvious that Wyllie had worked himself up into a furious state of indignation and could scarcely contain himself.

'Glynn, this time you have seriously interfered with the Court's administration of justice and unless I get an immediate apology in writing I will apply to the Judiciary for your instant dismissal'. I was still angry over the boy's public flogging, in particular my slowness reacting earlier than I did to stop the whole squalid business. I replied ' If you seriously believe that what you have just witnessed out there was an acceptable example of the administration of British justice you must be out of your Magisterial mind'.

He was clearly taken aback at this and it obviously never occurred to him that anyone would have the temerity to question whatever sentence he decided was appropriate.

'You have not been in this country for five minutes and are totally ignorant of the way the Courts operate and judicial procedures. I will not tolerate your unwarranted interference in my Court's proceedings. Nor am I willing to accept your ridiculous and public instruction to a Court official carrying out the duties I have assigned to him. Just who do you think you are?'

'I don't think, I know that I am an officer in the Colonial Service which enjoys a well deserved reputation for honest, lawful and corruption free administration of the Territories to which we have been assigned. I also know that what you have done this morning flies in the face of everything the Service stands for; in my view this is a matter of shame and concern.

'Oh, indeed and what precisely do you imagine you are going to do about it?'

'If I was that boy's father I wouldn't rest until the whole case, in every detail, together with witness statements, had been submitted to the Chief Justice with a request that you be removed from Judicial duties'. By now Wyllie was almost incandescent and he bellowed that I should leave his office immediately or he would have me thrown out – by whom was not immediately apparent. Back at the Department I had real problems coming to

terms with my anger and it didn't help when Aron filled me in
with the background details of the case. I had a shameful feeling
that I should have intervened earlier than I did with the thought
that some of the damage could have been avoided. What I found
hard to come to terms with was my inability to do anything
helpful other than tell Aron to contact the boy's father and get
him to take him to the Indian doctor for treatment for which I
would pay. Otherwise, they might treat him with traditional
medicine which would doubtless make matters worse.

It was obvious that Wyllie would do his utmost to make trouble
over this and a formal complaint over my behaviour could be
taken for granted. In anticipation I asked Aron to if he would
help the father to request a Case Stated from the Court to which
he was entitled as this would provide a detailed account of the
Court proceedings leading to the boy's conviction. Once this was
obtained it was evident from the record that:-

> There were no other witnesses to the arrest other than the
> Askari.

> The owners of the tricyle had not registered a complaint of
> theft.

> The Boy had pleaded 'Nimecosa' which translates to' I am
> at fault'

This should not have been accepted as an unequivocal plea of
guilty on a charge of theft of a tricycle; it could easily mean the he
was at fault for riding it.
   This was a first offence, the boy had never been in trouble
with police and no evidence was led of previous convictions.
   In the light of the above it could be argued that the conviction
was unsound and that the sentence of 10 strokes in a public
flogging was grossly excessive, given the evidence and the boy's
age.

Of course none of this would be much help in defense of my
actions in intervening in the execution of a punishment ordered

by a Magistrate but it might be accepted in mitigation of my actions. In the meantime I could only hope that, whatever complaint was made by Wyllie, I would be given an opportunity to submit a response. I might also argue that that given the rising anger of the crowd outside the Court my action might have helped avert a more serious situation developing. It was weeks before I had any information about the outcome. This took the form of an interview with the Provincial Commissioner who informed that my behaviour had been the subject of a formal complaint by the Magistrate to the Judiciary in Dar es Salaam. But that he was not in a position to release its contents at this stage. However, I was given the opportunity of explaining what prompted my actions at the time. This was received without comment other than the P.Cs. observation that all officers in the Provincial Headquarters are expected to work together as a team. He also let it be known that the Dodoma Town Council had submitted its own complaint over this case particularly about the excessive sentence; I suspected that Panjawni may have had some influence over this. When I asked the P.C. what I was expected to do his advice was do nothing. However, as I was leaving his office he called me back and said 'Glynn, there is one other thing, and this is in the strictest confidence, the date of Wyllie's impending long leave has been advanced at short notice and a new Magistrate will soon be in post.' I felt as though a ton weight had fallen off my shoulders and couldn't resist a smile but the P.C. warned me to watch my step. He went on to say that no one could predict how the people in the Secretariat in Dar es Salaam might react to a situation like this, it was just possible that a 'Confidential Black' might appear on my Personal File, but he would do what he could to avoid this.

Walking back to the Department I was able to view the future in a more optimistic perspective and could set aside concerns I had about the possible termination of my probationary service. I had not discussed the details of this case with Wyn although she would have sensed that I had been going through a pretty worrying time. On the domestic front things had been going pretty well, Wyn had mastered enough Swahili to get the best out of the servants and the childrens' Swahili had blossomed, indeed the servants often chose the children as a line of communication to Wyn and I when putting forward requests. Under these arrangements Joseph, our House Boy had let it be known that he wished to take a wife and needed a loan to meet part of the bride price. Since the amount he needed seemed fairly modest we agreed to this and, on the appointed day, we all waited with interest to see what the new bride would look like. Joseph, who had been given the day off, failed to show up until late evening when he arrived pretty drunk without a wife but wearing a cow-boy outfit – tall hat, plastic waist coat, tasseled chaps, and, incongruously, plastic spurs fastened round his bare feet. In a more sober mood next morning he explained that, having had a few drinks in the bar, it became a toss-up between a wife and the this out-fit which he had spotted in the bazaar – the wife apparently lost out.

In general our situation was good, Wyn had got the house sorted out, our shipping baggage had arrived and Wyn had now got the house very comfortable with our cherished possessions in place and everything in good order. The children had settled nicely into the local school and Peter had made a full recovery. Philip had given us a scare by picking up a scorpion, which stung him on the thumb – he was rushed off to the local doctor in great pain, injected with novocaine and made a quick recovery. Wyn had taken up an appointment teaching at the local Aga Khan School which, though strange at first, she was beginning to enjoy. She had also made friends with a number of nieghbouring wives at various coffee mornings sometimes with surprising results. At one house she was astonished to hear loud tribal chanting coming from the bathroom. Inside was a huge African servant with enormous feet stomping up and down in a bath full of soapy water and the week's laundry. On another occasion the host turned out to be a German lady determined to let the servants and anybody else know that she was a member of the 'master race' not averse to fisticuffs when she thought the servants needed it. At another coffee morning the host had broken with tradition of only employing men servants by employing a Wagogo girl in a black dress, white cap and apron reminiscent of pre-war Lyons Corner House. The results were less than spectacular as the seemed to have no idea what she was supposed to do.

Back at the Department the the staff awaited with some concern to see how the things might develop following my interview with the Provincial Commissioner. I called Panjawani, Aron and Jonathan into my office and explained that the dispute with the Magistrate had been settled and that we could all get on with our work without having to worry too much about the Resident Magistrate; I could not of course tell them of Wyllie's impending departure.

Mr. Panjawani seemed surprised, puzzled and relieved, to hear this and actually broke into a smile – a very rare event – saying that he had heard from the Court Clerk that I was to be dismissed. Apparently Wyllie had been putting it about that I was to have my probationary appointment terminated having convinced himself that there could be no other outcome to his formal complaint. His departure took place as anticipated and his replacement was a young Australian lawyer who proved to be a refreshing change. We soon established a good working relationship and, other duties permitting, he was kind enough to advise me on my preparatory studies aimed at getting me through my law examination. Now that the department had a driver and vehicle I was able to carry out a limited safari programme within which I managed to carry out inspections in the major townships within the Province. With the help of the Agricultural Officer and the Public Works Department the waste ground in front of the Department had been laid out with a stone border and planted with suitable plants and trees, the later designed to provide some shade. In addition hard standing and an open shelter had been built at the side of the office for the truck. With Maloda in charge a similar tidying up operation was carried out by the Messengers and Sweepers at the Labour Transit Centre. My Swahili was slowly improving but as I had no flare for languages I still had a considerable way to go before I could realistically hope to pass the Advanced Level written and oral examinations.

All things taken into account I was beginning to enjoy my assignment. Africa was proving to be a fascinating experience and working with Africans had turned out to be much easier than I had been led to expect.

COMPLAINTS AND DISPUTES

A substantial part of the Departments day to day operations involved dealing with complaints over employment issues. These mostly concerned Africans complaining against their Asian or European employers, usually about alleged unpaid wages, unlawful dismissals, accidents at work where compensation was due and rarely physical violence. Alternatively, the complaints came from employers over issues such as workers failing to complete tasks, desertion, damage to property and theft. Aron as Labour Inspector dealt with all these in the first instance and was very good at conciliation and would often secure an amicable settlement From time to time a situation would arise in which I had to intervene, sometimes when Aron felt he had run out of ideas or in cases where the complainant, usually European, demanded that they should be dealt with by a Labour Officer. Under these arrangements I was exposed to an aspect of human relations with surprising outcomes, particularly in dealing with disputes between employers (usually the Memsahib) and African domestic servants.

In the ordinary course of events all that was needed was a careful explanation of the legal position in the context of the Employment Ordinance and related legislation. However, in disputes between Memsahibs and servants it was often the case that a fair amount of anger and emotion crept into the equation and rational outcomes were not easily secured. Experience in dealing with these complaints revealed who were good and sensible employers and those who had a record of constant trouble with staff and an inability to retain staff for any length of time. It was also the case that servants, with poor employment records and likely to cause trouble, were also known and of course this background knowledge would be taken into account in trying to get a settlement. In seeking employment cooks, house-boys dhobi's and shamba-boys would register at the Department and when vacancies were notified they would be put in touch with potential employers. Central to this system was the ability of employees to show, through recommendations from former employers, that they possessed the necessary experience and good character. 'Chits' bearing this information from former employers were a valuable indicator of likely success in the job concerned and were greatly treasured by those who earned them. However, over time this value was sometimes realised through other means and chits were sold or loaned between employees so much so that there authenticity was often questioned. Ali could become Juma overnight if the Chit so required and many Africans found it easier to change their name than change their socks – where worn. Complicating the issue still further was what might be described as the 'Memsahib's Revenge'. Close examination of the Chits, which were invariably drafted in English, revealed expressions such as:-

'Juma has worked for me for two months and deserves a good berth – preferably a wide one.'

' Mohamed works well under superstition.'

'Ali is friendly and has taking ways.' Or, even less subtly-

'Pius tries hard but is a bit thick.'

Of course the Memsahibs themselves did not have to produce Chits as to their suitability as employers and Africans were not slow to point out this anomaly.

With a view to regularising the situation someone in Labour Headquarters introduced a system of Employment Record Books in which the employees identification, work experience and recommendations from employers, could be formally recorded. Based on experience in Kenya in dealing with the 'Mau Mau' insurrection, where polaroid photographs were used for identification purposes, similar photographs were include in the Record Books. A batch of Record Books, polaroid cameras and film was issued to every Labour Office in the Territory. The Books were issued complete with photograph, a duplicate copy of which was retained for record purposes. A rather surprising and unlooked for side effect emerged, however, when it was seen that the negative showed a black person as a white person although the features remained unchanged of course. The idea of being shown as a white person proved very attractive to some Africans and they became more important than the actual picture in the Record Book. Mainly because of the price, Sgs.5 and the fact that many employees were not anxious to be positively identified the scheme failed and had to be abandoned; it was uncertain what use was found for the cameras. But it would not have surprised me if some enterprising Asian had taken the lot and set up a profitable business selling negatives.

Dismissed domestic servants would congregate outside the office waiting to register their complaints and would discuss in detail their version as to why their services were terminated. Usually a light-hearted view was taken of these events and descriptions of the Memsahibs involved were often the subject of much ribaldry. They had their own names for different employers, not always complimentary, and claimed to know everything that was going on in the household they had just left, particularly their employers domestic, social and sexual behaviour. How much of what was claimed had a basis in truth was a matter for speculation. Although my Swahili was not really up to much of what was said I could sometimes get the gist of it and had to get Maloda to move them away as I would know many of the people under discussion and searching insights into their personal lives, even though much of it was pure fantasy was not something I wished to have at the back of my mind. A typical example of this kind of stuff was a house-boy dismissed for drinking his employers gin and filling up the bottle with water. Unfortunately for him Dodoma water was still cloudy even after being double filtered and the offence was easily detected. He had no complaints about his dismissal as such but claimed that the gin bottle was only half full and the employer had deducted the price of a full bottle from his wages. Whilst waiting to register his complaint another house-boy was regaling other complainants with the story that his Bwana and Memsahib had suddenly cleared all the furniture out of the main bedroom and that every night they had an 'ngoma' (tribal dance) with loud music. The dance took the form of quickly spinning round very fast clinging to each other and stone cold sober. This unlikely story found a basis of truth when, shortly afterwards, the couple concerned put on a very professional display of dancing on roller skates at a Gala Night at the Club; a performance which implied extensive rehearsal. Behind all these stories was the conclusion that when Juma, Ali, or whoever, was finishing his duties for the day and turning down the beds, tucking in the mosquito nets and spraying the bedroom against mosquitoes etc. He would also carefully draw the curtains making sure that there was a slight but unobtrusive gap left through which he could subsequently view whatever may be going on in the bedroom.

Not all disputes between employers and their domestic servants were easily resolved, particularly in cases where some cherished object or expensive piece of glass or crockery was broken. The difficulty arose when the employer set a value on the object and insisted on making substantial reductions in the servants wages. Assessing the value of such objects was always difficult, seldom was the property insured and more often the item concerned was of special personal intrinsic value. Sometimes the Memsahib would claim that the item was Wedgwood or Limoge and, although the broken item was seldom produced, there seemed to be no satisfactory basis around which a settlement could be achieved. It was invariably the case that if the deductions were set too high and over a long repayment period the employee would simply disappear. What was particularly tiresome were disputes which arose when the employer was preparing to go home on long leave and, in lieu of wages would offer the staff unwanted items of clothing or household utensils. The servants would quite rightly claim that they were entitled to wages in cash as the law prescribed whilst the Memsahib would argue that the items offered far exceeded in value the wages due. Such disputes often turned emotional the Memsahib claiming that servants were ungrateful no matter how well they were treated they scarcely ever said thank you. What was seldom recognised was that there was no such word as 'thanks' in the Chigogo tribal dialect and that, in terms of native law and custom the occasions when they were obliged to help their nieghbours was clearly understood – gratuitous charity didn't come in to it. Aron was told not to get into this kind of argument but to insist that wages when due were paid in cash.

Some disputes seemed to go on interminably without hope of settlement. One that troubled me for weeks was a claim for wages between a local African farmer and a Somali cattle trader. At some time in the past a verbal agreement had been reached in which the farmer would take care of five donkeys whilst the Somali owner visited the Coast Region. The farmer claimed that he had been promised wages for grazing the donkeys and generally taking care of them. The Somali claimed that wages were never involved but if the donkeys bred the farmer could keep the foals. The situation was further complicated by the fact that there were only three donkeys when the Somali returned, the farmer claiming that one died from snake bite and the other was taken by hyenas; the Somali claimed they had been sold. The problem was further complicated by the fact that both sides could call any number of witnesses to support their case and the hearing of so called evidence was becoming an enormous waste of time. I mentioned the problem to the Dodoma District Officer, with whom I had been taking Swahili lessons and after a moments thought he advised that I should inform both parties that I wished to see their grazing permits before we could proceed any further with the case; I never saw them again.

PART 4

JOSEPH BEWITCHED

One Sunday afternoon two Wagogo came to the house and through the servants asked if they could speak to me as a matter of urgency. Thinking that this was just another labour problem or complaint of some sort I would normally ask them to come to the Department in normal working hours. To do otherwise would lead to a constant stream of people coming directly to the house at any time of day. However, the two middle-aged men raised a problem which required immediate attention. It turned out that they were the elder natural, as opposed to tribal, brothers of Joseph the Overseer / Dresser employed at the Labour Transit Centre who needed my help because of special difficulties. They reported that there had been some trouble at the Transit Centre and Joseph had been taken away by the Police who were holding him in a cell at the police station. When asked what Joseph had been up to they explained that he had been bewitched and had tried to kill a small boy who according to Joseph had put a spell on him. Apparently Joseph had been screaming and cursing and had chased the boy with an axe but the boy had managed to escape. I said that this was a matter for the Police and that a cell was the best place for him until he could get medical help, so why come to me. They replied 'Well Bwana, this is an African problem and the police will not be able to help. What Joseph needs is African medicine and if he is not treated soon he will die'. I asked what exactly did they expect me to do and they urged that I use my influence to get Joseph released so that they could take him to a good 'Mchawe' – Witch Doctor.

I could see all kinds of problems with this but agreed to discuss the matter with the local Police Superintendent to see what might be done. At the Police Station Joseph was in a cell fastened by his hands and feet to an iron bed and showing every sign of violence, sweating profusely, eyes rolling and struggling to get loose. He failed to recognise me, or his two brothers, and was making a kind of low pitched chattering noise which suggested that he was out of his mind. The Superintendent explained that in cases like this the Medical Officer would be called to certify him and arrangements would then be made for his transfer to the mental asylum wing of the Prison Hospital. The brothers were very despondent on hearing this and made it clear that they knew European medicine would not work in a case like Joseph's and that he would certainly die. I explained that I did not think that there was much we could safely do but I agreed to have a word with the Medical Officer and let him know their views.

The next morning Joseph was quieter, doubtless because he was exhausted from all the struggling the previous day. The Medical Officer, who I knew fairly well, explained that the medical evidence was quite clear and that Joseph was temporarily out of his mind even though he was tranquil and asylum treatment was the likely option in such cases. He accepted that in cases of witch craft of which he had little experience it was sometimes the case that the patient did not respond to treatment and might relapse into a coma and eventually die.

The next day the brothers appeared at the Department to inform me that Joseph was now quiet but would not be admitted to the Prison Hospital for about a week so there was a good chance to get him treated if I could get him out. When asked what they would do with him they said that there was a good Mchawe at mile 15 along the Kongwa road who had dealt with cases like Joseph's before and he would cure him. They again pleaded that I should get him out as this was Joseph's only chance. My reaction was that this was essentially a police and medical case and it would be dangerous for me to intervene in a situation which I didn't fully understand. The brothers refused to accept this and set up a vigil outside the Office and later outside my house. The next morning they were still there so I called in at the police station to see how Joseph was progressing and found him walking about in his cell wearing handcuffs but failing to recognise me. In discussing the options with the Superintendent he pointed out that, so far as the police were concerned, Joseph had not committed a crime and no charge sheet had been made out against him. He went on to say that he could release him but only if I certified in writing that I accepted full responsibility for any of his actions or subsequent behaviour.

This called for a judgement that I was ill equipped to make in the light of my limited experience in Africa and in particular the darker side of African witch craft. Commonsense dictated that I should leave well alone and let Joseph's problems be taken care of by conventional means. On the other hand, I had a high regard for Joseph who was hard working, honest, cheerful and friendly and was doing a good job in the day to day management of the Transit Centre. He also had a nice young family living with him at the Centre and their future had to be considered. The thought of him languishing in a prison asylum with an uncertain medical outcome, so far as treatment was concerned, was a real worry and if the worst happened I would have serious difficulties trying to come to terms with my failure to try an alternative. The alternative in this case meant placing reliance on the effectiveness of traditional medicine, with all the uncertainties associated with that, notwithstanding the assurances of the two brothers and their conviction that this was an African problem requiring an African solution.

After careful thought and in some trepidation I agreed to sign for Joseph on the understanding that if traditional medicine failed I could bring him back to the Police and conventional treatment. Accompanied by the brothers we collected Joseph, who seemed to have little understanding of what was happening, and with his hands tied behind his back we took him out to find the Mchawe. About 15 miles along the Kongwa Road we left the truck with Abdullah at the roadside and walked about two miles through the bush. The Mchawe turned out to be a rather dirty, toothless grey-haired, old man who seemed partially blind living in a mud and wattle hut which seemed on the point of collapse As we approached he slowly got to his feet but offered no greeting and seemed to regard us with some suspicion as one of the brothers explained Joseph's situation. The witch doctor's response was to slowly circle Joseph but without touching him as he muttered a few words in Chigogo. He then entered the hut and returned carrying a half coconut shell containing some oily liquid which he sprinkled on Joseph's bare feet and carefully watched for some reaction. So far as I could see nothing happened but the Mchawe seemed satisfied and he started to negotiate with the brothers about terms ignoring me completely. The outcome was that he agreed to treat Joseph, claiming this to be a very difficult case, and that he would need Sgs.40 and the brothers would have to provide Joseph's food. One of the brothers had brought a kikapu containing food, mostly maize meal and two chupas containing milk or water. Between them they could only raise Sgs. 15 and I was required to make up the balance. After further discussion Joseph was left sitting on a mat with his hands still tied and his left ankle tied to the door post of the hut.; he seemed to be totally unaware of his surroundings and did not respond to the brothers efforts to say goodbye. On the way back the brothers assured me that one of them would visit Joseph each day as they owned a bicycle and they would keep me informed of any developments. Both seemed content with the arrangements at the Mchawe's and were confident that a cure would soon be achieved. I must confess that I could see no grounds for such optimism.

Two days later the brothers appeared at the Department to ask for my assistance. They claimed that the Mchawe was no longer willing to treat Joseph whose condition was unchanged and there was some suggestion that the Mchawe didn't like the involvement of a Mzungu (a European). Asked what they now proposed to do they assured me that there was an even better Mchawe about 14 miles south of Dodoma who specialised in dealing with bewitched people and, although he was more expensive, he was probably the best hope if Joseph was going to be cured. So far as money was concerned they would arrange to borrow this and Joseph would repay it when he returned to work. What they needed from me was transport to collect him and get him to the new Mchawe. It seemed to me that my worst fears were beginning to materialise all too quickly and my instincts were to get him back to the police forthwith. I asked Maloda if he had ever heard of the Mchawe the brothers were now proposing and after some discussion with them he said he had heard he was good but did not know anyone who had used him. I told the brothers that this was their last chance and that if there was no real improvement in the next three days I would return Joseph to the Police without further argument.

On the basis of their flimsy assurances and the understanding that my involvement would cease after two days, we picked up Joseph who seemed to be in some sort of trance and delivered him to the new Mchawe. This one seemed to be an altogether different proposition compared with the first one and he gave us a friendly greeting seemingly glad to see us. He was a tall distinguished looking Mgogo with Nilotic features wearing a clean white kanzu a hand stitched kofia (hat) and leather sandals. The first thing that struck me about him was his air of calm authority and intelligence. His hut was in good shape with a metal roof and the compound had recently been swept. After detailed discussion with the two brothers, in which he asked a number of questions, he examined Joseph, who still had his hands tied, looking into his eyes, pulling down his eye lids and feeling his pulse. His conclusion was that he could probably help but it may take time and it would cost Sgs.60 plus the cost of 'dawa' – traditional medicine. On this basis we left Joseph sitting on a stool in front of the hut staring into space and seemingly oblivious of his surroundings.

Four days later the brothers reappeared in fairly cheerful mood claiming that Joseph's treatment had now been completed and he was now ready to return home. I found this difficult to believe but was somewhat relieved to hear that there had been some progress and we went out to collect him. When we arrived we found Joseph sitting on a stool talking to the Mchawe and at first glance he seemed quite normal. He recognised me immediately and carefully getting to his feet said 'Jambo Bwana' but expressed no surprise to find me there. The day before one of the brothers had brought him clean cloths and having had a shave he was looking pretty much his old self, but something fundamental had changed. Instead of the cheerful, noisy self confident person I had come to know, Joseph was now quiet, reserved, and spoke in a low voice with some hesitation as though searching for words. Nevertheless I was astonished and greatly relieved at this outcome and thanked the Mchawe for his help which had proved so effective. His somewhat surprising reply was that he could only work with God's help, which particular God he had in mind was a matter for speculation. The brothers seemed to take this new and welcome situation for granted and after some discussion with the Mchawe about payment for 'dawa' we were soon on our way back to Dodoma and Joseph's family who were delighted to see him. It wasn't long before Joseph resumed his normal duties at the Transit Centre and he seemed to fit in as though he had never been away. But he was certainly not the same Joseph as there seemed to have been a complete personality change since he spoke slowly in a low voice and could seldom be seen to smile. He had no problems recognising people and was able to carry out his Overseer / Dresser duties as heretofore. He moved about fairly cautiously, as though he had been injured in some sort of accident. Some days later I asked him about the treatment he received at the Mchawe's and without comment he raised the back of his shirt to reveal the most horrific burn scars on his back which were not yet healed. It was as though someone had placed a red hot poker on his back a number of times and this more or less was the only treatment he had received apart from some herbal drink to ease the pain. I took him to see the local doctor to have his back properly treated and explained to him what had happened. In a general discussion about the case he explained that Joseph had undergone treatment not dissimilar in intention to electric shock therapy which was the current vogue in modern medicine in dealing with mental patients suffering from acute depression. How such an appalling variant on this modern treatment had found its expression in the heart of the Africa bush remains a mystery. The overall outcome was that Joseph's back eventually healed and thereafter he settled down to his job and new life without further incident. Commenting on this back at the Department, Maloda said the Mchawe had turned Joseph into an 'mgeni' – a stranger.

SAFARI TO SINGIDA

I had a feeling that something unusual had happened when Panjawani, my Chief Clerk, followed by Aron the Labour Inspector, came walking to meet me both looking slightly worried.

'Good morning, is there something wrong?'

'The Provincial Commissioner wants to see you as soon as possible.'

'Any idea what its about?'

'No Sir,' both of them managing to avoid my eyes. 'Right then I will go straight across to the Boma and find out.'

Panjawani placed his finger against his nose and said that it might be something to do with Singida – as though he had been in touch with some mystic oracle. I knew him well enough to realise that he had probably been in touch with his Asian colleague who was the P.C.s' Chief Clerk.

'Aron what do you think?'

'I don't know Sir, but perhaps I should get the Driver and Messenger lined up for a safari.' As usual both were better informed than me operating on their separate Asian and African networks.

Approaching the Boma, which housed the Provincial Headquarters, reminded me of Beu Geste because of its fort like construction. It was built by the Germans, about the turn of the century, when Tanganyika was German East Africa. It took the form of a large square granite fortress with thick high walls, a watch tower at each corner and only one entrance in the form of a solidly built wooden main gate with a deep well in the centre of the court yard. The whole edifice was designed to withstand any form of siege indefinitely and with machine guns mounted in the watch towers defenders would have been able to inflict any amount of damage to invaders without much risk to the German occupiers. The Provincial Commissioner's office commanded an excellent view of the North / South Road (literally Cape to Cairo) and running East to West through the centre of the town, the Central Railway line linking Dar es Salaam on the Indian Ocean to Lake Victoria in the heart of Africa. There was a lot of activity in the court yard as a group of Asian, Arab and Somali, traders were viewing a collection of elephant tusks, rhino horns, lion and leopard skins and other game trophies. Most of the stuff had been confiscated from poachers and was now due to be auctioned by the District Commissioner.

The Provincial Commissioner's office was a reflection of its former German occupiers with fine game trophies, particularly buffalo, adorning the walls and heavy wooden furniture including a desk which might have been designed for the Kaiser. The P.C. was closely examining some drawings of African tribal heads produced by his son – a budding young artist.

'Ah, Glynn, what brings you here?'

Good morning Sir, I was told that you wished to see me.'

'Yes, let me think – something to do with Singida. That's it, the District Officer seems to be worried about some labour problems at the new dam they are building at Kirondatal. Been up there recently?'

'No Sir, but I was in Singida about two months ago carrying out inspections.'

'Good, the D.O. will put you in the picture. I believe the work is being carried out by the Water Development Department and that they have got themselves into some kind of trouble with local people. I would like you to go up there as soon as you can as these things can turn into real problems fairly quickly.'

As I was leaving the P.C's office he called me back saying 'I should keep an eye open for the Wasandawe, can be tricky, so watch your step'.

It didn't sound so bad apart from the fact that I had no idea where Kirondatal was and was even less well informed about the Wasandawe, whatever it or they were. Back at the Department preparations were well in hand for a safari. Abdullah had driven the truck on to the hard standing at the side of the office and, with the help of the Messengers, was laying out the stores ready for inspection. In the office Panjawani had all the inspection files on undertakings in Singida laid out and Aron was sorting out the Local Purchase Orders and a cash Imprest to meet anticipated subsistence allowances for the staff and for fuel and other items we might need on safari.

'Mr. Panjawani do we know anything about Kirondatal – has anybody been there?'

'No sir, we don't have a file on it.'

'Aron, what do you know about the Wasandawe?'

'I have never been up there but they are the tribe north of Singida.'

'Right, lets have a look at the map and try to work out how much further north as there will be no fuel beyond Singida and there may not be any there.' From the map it looked as though Kirondatal was about 18 miles north east of Singida and the road was shown as a bush track which fizzeled out five miles out of Singida. Judging from the map, it was obvious that there would be no place to sleep at Kirondatal in which event camping equipment would be necessary and I asked Panjawani to open the store and get the stuff laid out by the truck. At this point Maloda came into the office asking for his subsistence allowance, but past experience had shown that any advance before the safari would be spent early and he would be seeking a loan to see him through the rest of the trip. Asked if he had been to Kirondatal, he claimed to have been there with Bwana Robson – Gibson 'Zamani' – a long time ago. Asked where they slept he said 'in the truck'. Aron had his doubts about this and Panjawani was shaking his head in disbelief. The trouble with Maloda was that he claimed to have been every where no matter how remote and reliance on these assertions had certainly led to trouble in the past – however, we should see.

I gave instructions for the vehicle and equipment to be ready for inspection in half an hour and in the meantime slipped home to get my safari gear. Wyn would always prepare a flask and sandwiches to get me through the first day but after that it would be canned food or whatever could be found on route. It always surprised me how little notice seemed to be needed before the team were ready to start. Aron needed ten minutes to gather his gear, usually a blanket, a flask and his bible. Abdullah the driver would bring a small kikapu containing food which would satisfy his Muslim requirements and his prayer mat. Maloda would get a message to his family out in the bush and would only bring his panga. Elio and Rumigo's arrangements were never clear since we picked them up at the Transit Centre on the edge of town; usually all they carried between them was a throwing stick and their pangas. Checking the vehicle and equipment was an important and necessary routine which Abdullah was reluctantly coming to accept. The vehicle had reached the point in its life when anything could happen since most of its mileage had been done on some of the worst roads in the Territory. The drill was to lay out the all the safari equipment on the hard standing outside the office, tent, poles, fly-sheet, mosquito net, ground sheet, camp bed, wash stand and chair. So far as the truck was concerned, tool kit, tyre-levers, pump, patches, gaiters, jack and spare wheel plus 'U' bolts for the suspension. Jerry cans for petrol, water, drinking water, oil etc. The detailed list was checked first by Aron then by me before loading.

It is always the small things that get left behind, matches, first aid kit, lamps, cooking pots etc.

In less than a mile from the centre of Dodoma we were in the African bush much of which hadn't changed since the time of the flood. The MMBA as it was commonly referred to – Miles and Miles of Bloody Africa. The Greek garage was the last evidence of commercial activity. After that there were a few typical Gogo shambas i.e. traditionally built rectangular houses of mud and wattle with a low narrow door, no windows but the design included a small round hole in the gable end through which the inhabitants could spit. Tradition dictated that there should be no flue or chimney so that when fires were lit smoke poured out under the eaves or through the roof creating the impression that the house was on fire. The shamba surrounding the house or 'tembe' to give it its Gogo name, was a cleared patch of bush on which maize, millet and cassava was grown dependent on the uncertain rainfall. Children, chickens, goats, dogs and partially blind old people, were the hazards to look out for when driving past shambas but Abdullah, unless told otherwise, would invariably fail to slow down notwithstanding.

Beyond the shambas there was nothing but barren semi desert scrub-land of miombo and acacia trees and dense thorn bushes interspersed with tall rocky outcrops and uphorbia trees, the home of hyrax and baboons often much in evidence and, from time to time but rarely seen in daylight, lions and leopard. The Bahi Depression to which we were headed lay about 50 miles due west and some way beyond that Manyoni were we planned to spend the night. Gathering speed as we left the shambas there were no obvious dust trails in the distance so it looked as though ours was the only vehicle headed that way and, although there had been short rains in other parts of the Province the road was bone dry. We were of course creating our own dust cloud behind the truck and, despite all our efforts to seal against it, thick cocoa like dust was getting into the cab. With three of us sitting in the cab it was a tight uncomfortable squeeze, but Aron was too senior to sit in the back with the messengers. He was a poor traveler at the best of times and the combination of heat, a badly corrugated road which threatened to shake the truck to pieces, and dusts, would usually cause him to vomit if I didn't stop the truck about every 50 miles to give him a break. Abdullah had now settled the truck in top gear and we were making good if noisy progress at about 40 miles an hour.

Approaching Bahi the road drops down about 800 feet into a depression which stretches about 40 miles ahead until it reaches the escarpment on top of which is the plateau and Manyoni our first scheduled stop. During the rains the depression, which is part of the Great Rift Valley, fills up with water to a depth of about three feet. It attracts a wide range of migratory bird life including knob nosed geese, spurwing geese, egrets and various species of duck. The road is built up for that reason and in the dry season forms a causeway with an occasional wooden bridge over culverts to allow an even flow of water either side. Six miles into the depression is a dry riverbed, which has water just below the surface of the sand. Consequently there is green vegetation, palms and bamboo along the edges where monkeys and baboon could often be seen. Travelling over the causeway there were odd patches of shallow water indicating that the short rains had fallen to the north and some bird life was evident in the far distance.

Because of the narrowness of the causeway the road had been worn into two deep grooves caused by vehicles crossing in the rains and sinking into the soft mud. In the dry season these grooves set like concrete and steering was a matter of getting the front wheels in to the grooves and staying there, always hoping that no other vehicle would approach from the opposite direction. Above the rattle of the truck there was a sudden thumping noise on the roof of the cab indicating that the Messengers were calling for a halt. For the reasons mentioned above I was never keen to stop in the depression, apart from the problem of oncoming traffic, it was hot and fly ridden and it was always a relief to reach the escarpment and climb up into a cooler climate.

'Right Abdullah we had better stop and see what is bothering them.'

Before the truck had come to a halt Maloda was round to my side of the cab urgently trying to get the door open.

'Shauri gani' – whats the matter? 'Bwana, ndege kubwa sana huko' pointing to some scrub about 100 yards away and a fairly large bird. It seemed like some kind of stork, too big for a heron, all white feathers and standing about four feet high busy feeding on the edge of a small pool. I had never seen anything like it and asked Aron what it might be. He too claimed never to have seen a bird as big as this.

'Abdullah, what do you make of it?' After shading his eyes and staring at it for some time he replied 'Ndege tu' – its only a bird.

'Maloda, what is all the fuss about?' He swiftly replied that this was very good food and Bwana Robson-Gibson had shot plenty of these.

Robson–Gibson was one of my predecessors who, if Maloda was to be believed, spent most of his time shooting anything that moved. Abdullah, sensing that there may be something on had a quick change of mind and decided to support Maloda arguing that the bird would be good to eat. They were all waiting for me to get my gun from rack above me and hoping for some action. To the Wagogo fresh meat was like manna from heaven and from what the Messengers were saying to miss this opportunity would be the height of folly. They were well aware of the well established understanding that where an opportunity occurred any self respecting 'Bwana' would, when on safari, shoot small game or birds the meat from which would be shared amongst the safari team. Despite this, I remained to be convinced, first I rather liked the bird, it was strange and beautiful doing no harm to anyone and since no one could put a name to it there was the possibility that it might be protected. Perhaps more compelling was the knowledge that whilst I had a bird license this normally covered such things as duck, geese, or game birds such as guineafowl, sandgrouse etc. Shooting this might be difficult to justify if challenged – admittedly an unlikely event out here. On the other hand, my past performance was no guarantee that I would hit it even if I tried and a miss would be accepted as just another example of my unpredictable shooting.

'Right then, drive on about another 100 yards.' This always mystified Maloda but the conditions of my license prohibited shooting from less that 200 yards from any vehicle so some stalking would be necessary.

'The rest stay with the truck, Maloda come with me but be ready in case I only wound it.' 'Ndio, Bwana, lakini piga mzuri sana tafadali' – Yes sir but please shoot straight and don't miss it.'

We managed to get within about 80 yards without any disturbance although the bird was alert and watching us. I was using a Bruno 22 Magnum which had a good flat trajectory at this range and with an accurate shot plenty of power to ensure an instant kill. This was a one shot opportunity since there was no chance of my hitting the bird if it took flight. As I took aim I could sense Maloda behind me praying to 'Mungu' that for once I might 'Piga Kabisa'- get a good kill. The second I fired the bird moved, half turning to its right and crouching ready to take off with partly out stretched wings. However, I knew I had a hit as the bird was knocked off its feet falling backwards into the water. Maloda set off like a long dog knee deep in water and panga at the ready. Meanwhile the bird was thrashing about and eventually it managed to regain its feet and started to run but one wing was seriously damaged and dragging in the water. The driver and the other two messengers were now running at an angle to try to cut the bird off, Abdullah waving his knife. As a practicing Muslim he hoped to slit its throat before it died otherwise he would not be allowed to eat the meat. There was no way I could get in a second shot with Maloda between me and the bird and the others closing in nearer to the target. To see portly Abdullah really belting along notwithstanding the water struck me as extraordinary give his general idleness.

The bird was tiring quickly and it seemed just a matter of time before someone would reach it. Suddenly the bird stopped and turned on its aggressors, one wing extended and screeching as it ran at its persuers all of whom about faced and for a moment the bird was chasing them. It now became pure pantomime as Maloda and company scattered away from the bird which was still making a horrible screeching noise. I was now able to get in a quick second shot which dropped the bird in its tracks. From that moment on Abdullah lost all interest in the bird and splashed his way back to the truck wet and despondent. Maloda picked up the bird and carried it back when we could all get a close look at it. With all white plumage and long blue legs, but not web feet, it looked like a crested crane but was larger standing about four feet with a stork like yellow beak and feathered tufts over its bright yellow eyes. My first shot had broken the joint in its wing bone making flight and escape impossible; the second shot had hit it squarely in the breast killing it instantly. It was a beautiful bird and I was beginning to regret the whole episode, notwithstanding all the noises about it being 'Nyama muzuri' – good meat. I could have bought a couple of hens in Manyoni which would have provided just as good a meal without all this.

To make matters worse, judging from the discussion amongst the team, it was obvious that they had never seen a bird like this before and there seemed to be some doubt as to whether or not it could be eaten. Worse still, Abdullah, who was clearly disappointed about not being able to eat it, was now suggesting that it might be 'Bahati mbaya' In other words a bird like this could bring bad luck.

'Alright, lets get this sorted out.' Maloda did you tell me that Bwana Robson-Gibson shot plenty of these or not?' 'Perhaps he did Bwana.'

'Abdullah, did you or did you not tell me that a bird like this would be good to eat?'

'It's a bird Bwana and you can usually eat most birds.'

'So, what's all this about bad luck?'

'Well, I have never seen a bird like this before.'

Maloda who could see that I was really getting fed up about all this then said if we didn't eat it we could still use the feathers for making arrows.

'So, you really think its all right to kill a bird like this just for a few feathers?'

'Yes, Bwana, they really make good arrows.'

'Aron, what do you think about all this?'

'Well Sir, these people are Wagogo and it is well known that they are animals who will normally eat anything but now they are frightened because of what Abdullah said about bad luck.'

By now I was really annoyed, not least with myself for shooting against my better judgement – I was stuck like the ancient mariner with an unlucky bird that nobody wanted. It was now nearly five o-clock and we were still some miles from Manyoni where I planned to spend the night in the Government rest house.

'Right, I hear what you say about this bird and I know that what you said before I shot it was 'Wongo' – lies. If you think this bird is bad luck and that it might harm you I am sure that you will not want to sit in the truck with it. So, you can now walk to Manyoni and report to Aron at the Boma when you get there. If you are lucky he will then pay your night's subsistence allowance.' I then drove off with Aron who was always delighted when I took over the driving especially if Abdullah had to sit in the back, but now he was particularly pleased that Abdullah would have to walk. As we drove off with the bird in the back the Messengers were crowding round Abdullah who seemed due for a pretty hard time from the looks of it.

Just before we reached the escarpment we came up to three Wagogo women carrying head-loads of firewood to some shambas further down the road. I stopped the truck and waited for the dust to settle as they caught up with us. As we got out of the truck they stopped about twenty yards away to see what we wanted and if we planned to do them any harm. After the usual customary greetings they came closer and I was able to show them the bird in the back of the truck. Asked if they had ever seen a bird like this before they said yes. Asked if a bird like this was good to eat they said 'of course'. I asked if I gave them this bird which I had just shot would they eat this one.

'What do you want for it?'

'Nothing, this is a zawadi – a gift. The oldest woman, who may have been the senior wife, dropped her head load and quickly grabbed the bird beaming with delight. As we drove off there were shouts of 'Asanti' and 'Asante Sana' – thank you and thank you very much. Needless to say I was greatly relieved at this outcome and Aron couldn't wait to tell Abdullah and the rest of them that by then the bird had probably been cooked and eaten. To this day I have not been able to identify this bird and still have an uncomfortable feeling that shooting it was a singularly stupid thing to do. Were it not for its all white plumage it might have been a Saddle-Billed Stork which normally has a black head, neck and the underside of its wings. In size and shape it resembled a Crowned Crane but the absence of a crest and grey colouring ruled that out. A Black Stork seemed to be another alternative but the absence of black and grey markings made this unlikely; unless it was that rare possibility an albino specimen.

Driving up the escarpment proved uneventful although the road edges on the drop side had weathered away in some places and rock falls from above were sometimes still in the road.; edging round these called for some careful driving. Aron said it reminded him of the Katonka Gorge in the Southern Highlands Province up which two Nuns from a local Mission had been driving a Volkswaggon when a tyre burst. They had plenty of experience in changing wheels and promptly set about this but problems arose when an elephant came down the escarpment stopping about 40 yards away to weigh up the situation. It was obviously intent on trying to pass them even though there was a cliff rising above on one side and a 600feet drop on the other. At the sight of the elephant the Nuns jumped back into the car hoping that it might turn back but, waving its trunk and sniffing the air, the elephant simply carried on waiting. The Nuns then decided to carry on changing the wheel in the hope that they might reverse to a point where the elephant could squeeze past. Five minutes later the elephant decided it was time to pass and slowly approached and the Nuns quickly scrambled back in the car which was still jacked up. According to Aron God came down on the side of the Nuns, as the elephant decided to pass on the outside squeezing the car up against the cliff face, knocking it off the jack and pushing it back about five yards. After carefully balancing along the edge of the escarpment the elephant managed to get past and was not seen again. The Nuns subsequently managed to get the wheel replaced and safely completed their safari due to a combination of luck, courage and effective prayer.

As we reached the top of the escarpment the radiator was boiling so we stopped to let it cool down before topping up with more water. The view looking east wards from the top of the escarpment over the Bahi Depression was really impressive at that time of day. As the sun started to decline the bright African glare changed gradually into a warm pinkish glow changing slowly into purple shadows. Across the Depression cooking fires were being lit in scattered Gogo tembes which could be seen flickering in the distance and the sound of cattle bells and small stock could be heard as cattle and goats were herded into the safety of their bomas against the hazards of the night. Through the binoculars I could see the Messengers about three miles away just starting the walk up the escarpment. It would be dusk if not dark by the time they reached Manyoni.

From the top of the escarpment it was an easy drive to Manyoni town, at the centre of which was the Boma where the District Officer could be found. Convention required that all officials visiting Manyoni should call at the Boma and sign the District Book so as to give the District Officer notice as to who was in his area. The only person about when we arrived was the head messenger and a police Askari who would be the watchman for the night. In response to my enquiries as to the whereabouts of the D.O. he replied 'Hi Upo' meaning he was absent. I knew from previous experience that he preferred not to be disturbed after office hours so I drove to the Government Rest House where I would spend the night. I told Aron that we would be leaving for Singida at 7.30 in the morning and he agreed to pay the driver and messengers their subsistence allowance when they eventually arrived at the Boma. He and the rest of the team would have no problems finding friends to spend the night with but, having received their allowance, the first stop would be the pombe shop where they could get locally brewed beer 'Pombe' made from fermented maize.

Manyoni is a small Township established round the railway station where trains from the Coast or the Lakes would take on fuel and water. It has now developed into a trading and marketing centre where local produce such as cattle, small stock and food are sold or exchanged for other commodities. The main street is a collection of shops or 'dukas' usually owned by Asian traders (duka wallahs) with a reputation for driving a hard bargain with Africans trying to sell local produce such as hides and skins, honey, beeswax and gum-arabic. It was not unusual for an Mgogo, with a gallon of pure honey to sell, to be kept waiting most of the day whilst the duka wallah feigned indifference knowing that eventually the Mgogo would finally agree to exchange his honey for a small cash sum or a package of tobacco or snuff. Practices such as this did nothing to improve the relationships between Africans and Asians and over the years animosity between the two races have almost become the norm. It is difficult to resist the view that in the longer term the duka wallahs and their families would pay a heavy price for some trading actions which might be described as sharp practice.

ITIGI TRANSIT CENTRE

We drove out of Manyoni in the early morning after the usual vehicle check and filling up with petrol and water at the local duka. Abdullah and the Messengers seemed to be in good shape, the foot safari of the previous day notwithstanding. Some thirty miles west of Manyoni is the small village of Itigi where the Department maintains a Labour Transit Centre similar to the one in Dodoma and used by migrant workers seeking employment in the sisal estates in the Eastern Province. I had read the inspection reports on the Centre carried out by my predecessors but this would be my first visit and after an uneventful but hot and dusty journey we reached Itigi where Maloda was able to direct us to the Centre on arrival. My first impression was that it was seriously neglected, the compound was overgrown with weeds and the kitchen, water point and dispensary were un-swept, rubbish seemed to be everywhere. The rafters in the main sleeping block housed a colony of bats whose droppings covered the floor and the Centre was deserted.

'Aron, what do you make of this?'

'It's a disgrace sir, I have never seen a Transit Centre as bad as this, we must find the Over / Seer Dresser and find out what is going on.'

I agreed that Aron should go into the village and try to locate him, in the meantime I checked the inventory of stores and equipment that should be in the Overseer's possession. All the buildings were made of cement block with corrugated metal roofs and seemed to be in good condition. However, there was no trace of a four stance Latrine Block which according to the plan should have been alongside the Sleeping Block. A large patch of dried grass and shrubs covered the spot where it should have been and Maloda walked in looking for the foundations. It occurred to me that these were deep-pit latrines with a 12 foot drop so I warned him to take special care as he might disappear in very unpleasant circumstances. However he managed to locate the concrete stances which covered the top of the pits which confirmed that the Latrine Block had been there but the building itself had obviously been removed. Shortly afterwards Aron returned with a very scruffy elderly African sporting a badly torn dirty shirt and shorts with every evidence of a monumental hangover. Aron explained that this was Petros, the Overseer / Dresser and said to him 'Sema Jambo'. With some effort Petros said 'Jambo Bwana, U Hali Gani – Hello Sir, what condition are you in ?'

'Jambo Petros, I am in good condition but I think you are in deep trouble.'

Once the Store and Dispensary were unlocked and the inventory checked it was quickly apparent that most of the items were broken or missing, there were no drugs or dressings and the Sweeper, according to Petros, had run away taking some of the stores with him. It was also clear that the Transients Log Book had not been kept up to date Petros claiming that there had been no workers in transit for a very long time. There was enough evidence to justify Petro's instant dismissal but there were a number of issues which had to be cleared up before taking such a step.; not least the disappearance of the Latrine Block. Petros claimed that he had no idea what had happened to it but Maloda claimed that it would be somewhere in the village and volunteered to find it. True to his word he came back after a short interval with the news that it was being used by a Duka Wallah as a store. After a short inspection Aron confirmed that this was the case and brought back with him the Asian shopkeeper, Mr. Bamji, to offer an explanation.

'Mr. Bamji can you explain to me how you come to be in possession of a building that belongs to a Government Transit Centre?'

'Yes Sir, Petros sold it to me for Shgs 500.'

'Petros what do you have to say about this?'

'I cant remember, Bwana, but I don't think it was 500 Shillings.'

'How much do you think it was?'

'Perhaps a hundred but I have forgotten.'

'So you both admit in front of these witnesses, that this building which is Government property was sold by Petros and bought by Bamji for an amount which is still in dispute'. When I report this to the police you will be prosecuted and both go to prison, what do you have to say to that?'

There was silence for a moment then Petros said 'Nimecosa Bwana' – I am at fault'. 'Mr. Bamji, what do you have to say?'

'I am innocent, I bought this building in good faith it was Petros who offered to sell it.'

'Do you seriously believe that this building is the property of Petros, or is it, like all the other buildings in the Centre, the property of Government?' No reply.

'Mr Bamji, if you can prove that the building is the property of Petros and not the Government then you will have nothing to worry about. But if you can't prove that it is not the property of Government then you will surely go to jail. Do I make myself clear?'

Bamji, who was perspiring and clearly distressed responded by saying, 'Sir, you must help me. I am not a criminal and my family must not suffer because I made the mistake of believing Petros when he told me the building was being demolished'. I was anxious to get on to Kirondatal and did not want to waste time swearing a formal complaint at the local Police Station and getting statements from witnesses etc..

'Mr. Bamji, I have a duty to report this theft to the Police and this I will do when I come back through Manyoni in about a weeks time. What I advise you to do in the meantime is to hire workmen to dismantle the building and re-build it on its original site at the Centre. You must pay all labour costs and the costs of any materials and, if you do this promptly and well, I will also report this and you may then only get a fine and not a prison sentence.'

'Petros, you are suspended without pay with immediate effect pending the outcome of the court case, so remove any personal property immediately and hand over the keys to Elio who will stay as temporary caretaker until I return. If you are wise you will work with Mr. Bamji to remove and re-build the Latrine Block without pay and this might count in your favour.'

'Mr. Bamji, do you have anything further to say?'

'Sir, I promise it will be done, I will put the work in hand mara-moja, it will be properly completed before you return. As for Petros, he is now my enemy and I do not want him working with me or to see him ever again.'

As we left for Singida I was reflecting on this worrying situation and could not escape the feeling that these problems would not have arisen if the Centre had been subjected to more frequent and effective inspections. In some respects Petros was the victim of isolation and poor supervision. So far as Bamji's assurances were concerned, doubtless he would discuss the situation with his colleagues at the Jamat Khama where he would receive doubtful advice as to how to proceed. Even though he was obviously frightened, I would be surprised if his promise to rebuild ever really came to anything. A more likely scenario would be excuses about not being able to find workmen or difficulties over getting cement etc.. The worst case would be if he were persuaded to seek help from a local advocate which would be expensive and time-wasting without in any way affecting the outcome in the slightest. Leaving Elio in the position of caretaker / watchman with a subsistence allowance of Shgs. 100 could only be regarded as a stop gap solution since he was in no way qualified to run the Centre. On return to Dodoma, Aron would have to be assigned to Itigi to re-establish the Centre, liaise with the Recruitment Agents, hire daily paid labour to clean up the compound and buildings and investigate the disappearance of the Sweeper. In the meantime a replacement Overseer / Dresser would have to be recruited.

Travelling north from Itigi, the bush track joined the main Manyoni / Singida road which was built over an old defunct railway line linking Manyoni to Kiangiri. It was still a dirt road, mainly murram or red or black soil but for the most part it was straight and level with occasional bridges over dry riverbeds.

Like most of the Central Province roads it was badly corrugated and attempts by the local Roads Foreman to re-grade the road with mechanical grading machinery were few and far between. On a day to day basis reliance was placed on a team of Wagogo daily paid labourers pulling what amounted to a large sweeping brush about eight feet wide along the road leveling out the loose sandy surface. The bristles of this were cut from branches of the local bush which had to be replaced fairly regularly. Notwithstanding the slow pace at which the team moved along the road the brush generated a huge dust cloud which made it dangerous to overtake and it usually required lots of hooting on the truck's horn to get the team to stop and move over. Passing such a team was always an occasion for much ribaldry and cries of 'Shillingi Moja' (one shilling) from Maloda evoked some pretty crude responses from the team. My Swahili was not really up to this but according to Aron this had something to do with the fact that the local Road Foreman was an active pederast.

About forty miles after leaving Itigi I called a halt at a small roadside African owned 'duka' to give Aron a break and see what might be available by way of refreshment. It never ceased to surprise me how often it was possible to find cold coca-cola in the most unlikely up-country situations. This place was no exception and from a battered paraffin driven refrigerator it was possible to buy ice cold bottled beer, or, the Messengers favourite, Fanta Orange. Something safe to eat was another matter. If I was lucky I could buy bananas or better still ripe Paw-Paw. On the other hand the team, who probably had a full set of parasites anyway, seemed able to eat anything even though it was cooked in the most unappetizing circumstances, without any side effects at all. During the break Aron said that it was somewhere round here that the porters carrying Dr. Livingstone's embalmed body from Chitambo, near lake Bangwelo where he died, to Bagamoyo on the East African Coast opposite Zanzibar, ran into trouble. The old slave route crossed from Unyamwezi into Ugogo about here and legend has it that the Wagogo Chiefs held up the porters demanding 'Hongo' – traditional gifts for allowing strangers to cross over Ugogo tribal land. In Aron's view this was unforgivable since the porters, who were undertaking an epic foot safari, were poor and almost destitute. From my limited experience of the Wagogo this didn't surprise me at all and it was probably factors such as this which led to Aron's poor opinion of the Wagogo in general. Aron, who gained his primary education at a Livingstone Mission School in Nyasaland had been taught to revere the courage of Livingston's African companions, Susi and Juma, without whose efforts and dedication his body would never have reached the coast. It was thanks to them that the dust of David Livingstone finally reached a place of honour in Westminster Abbey in London.

We were still making good time and I expected that we would be in Singida before nightfall. We were still travelling along the old rail track which had been built by an Italian settler who had been attracted to this area by the possibility of extensive cattle ranching and the prospect of gold mining. During the Second World War he had been confined in an Internment camp for German and Italian nationals whose properties had been taken over by the Government appointed Custodian of Enemy Property. After the war the British Government invested some £35 million in a poorly planned and ineffectively administered scheme for growing ground nuts aimed at alleviating the chronic post war shortage of vegetable oils. The scheme failed spectacularly and some £25 million was totally wasted. During this enterprise the Italian's railway line was removed and re-laid to link the Central line to Kongwa where the ground nuts were supposed to be produced.

The country was an unchanging vista of semi-desert thorn scrub interspersed with acacia and miombo trees and the very odd baobab trees. The flat plain being broken by rocky outcrops and frequent termite hills often reaching a height of fifteen feet or more. The bush was almost impenetrable but there were occasional clearings created by bush fires or Wagogo peasant farmers operating an ancient 'slash and burn' form of agriculture. Notwithstanding the hot dry climate there was no shortage of bird life such as ground hornbills, cape doves, hoopoes and cattle egrets. Occasionally, Paradise Wydah birds with their long fluttering tails could be seen and towards evening flocks of helmeted guinea fowl, running at ground level scratching for seeds, were evident in the undergrowth. Bird song was not much in evidence except for the 'go away' bird, whose distant call inviting us to go away was almost as commonplace as the call of the cape doves. Rarely, the urgent twittering call of the black throated 'Honey Guide' bird might be heard. Wagogo honey gatherers would follow the bird knowing it would lead them to beehives in the bush. They would respect natures rule that when the bird led them to a hive they would leave part of the honey comb as the bird's reward. Gogo mythology had it that if the bird did not get its reward next time it would lead them to a hive with a snake in it.

Suddenly there was an ominous clattering from the rear end of the truck and the messengers were thumping on the cab roof calling for a halt. Having stopped to examine the problem it soon became clear that the leaf spring suspension on the rear near side of the back axle had collapsed and would have to be fixed. With a truck this old and the badly corrugated road surface this was hardly surprising and this was a problem we had faced before. For this reason we carried spare 'U' bolts to replace the broken ones and it was a straight forward job to jack up the rear wheel, remove it and then fix the spring. This was a situation where Maloda came into his own as he had the interest and potential to become a useful mechanic given encouragement. Abdullah the driver held on to the view that his job was simply driving and should something go wrong someone else would have to fix it. On this occasion, further examination revealed that one of the secondary leaf springs had actually broken and the problem was to clamp it back in position until it could be replaced. I had read somewhere that this problem is easily dealt with by old Africa hands who would shoot and skin a zebra and, whilst the hide was still 'green' cut it in strips and bind these tightly round the spring. As the skin dries out it sets tight like an iron bandage round the leaf spring and will take any amount of punishment. Solutions along these lines sound pretty good when they are discussed by safari clientele on the verandah of the New Stanley Hotel in Nairobi but in the middle of the Central Province it is not without its limitations. The only thing I could shoot would probably be a giraffe, which would certainly delight Maloda and company, but in practical terms would require an extensive foot safari and was clearly out of the question. While we were working on the truck a large group of Wagogo came out of a track in the bush and crossed the road just in front of us. They were evidently returning from some kind of ceremony or party. Judging from the noise from ululating women and the singing it seemed that a fair amount of drinking had been taking place. The men were all in traditional Gogo tribal dress having painted their bodies with red ochre and sheep fat, long hair platted in pigtails, ears fully extended with copper weights and carrying spears or pangas. The women too were dressed for the occasion, some in bright coloured cotton kangas but more often in goat-skin skirts with uncovered breast and plenty of beads and copper wire armlets and anklets. There were many friendly greetings in Chigogo between them and the messengers and it was obvious that they had all been having a good time. A group of four middle-aged women stood in the monsoon ditch at the side of the road and lifting their skirts started to urinate whilst still standing. They were grinning at us and shouting some rude remarks, which I gathered, were intended for me. The urine was splashing down their legs making rivulets in the dust and soaking through the bands of copper wire used to decorate their ankles. I suddenly found myself blushing in response to their shouting and obscene

Typical Wagogo Tribesman
Dressed for an Ngoma - (Dance)
Labour Department in the background

gestures which were clearly directed at me. My own team was really enjoying this and I don't think they had seen anyone blush before and were quite intrigued by the whole business; Maloda commented that I was changing colour like a chameleon.

AN UNLIKELY IMPOSTER

We reached Singida just as it was going dark, the dukas in the main street were lit by oil lamps and trading was still in progress although there seemed to be fewer people about than usual. After receiving their subsistence allowance the team dispersed to find a meal and arrange their overnight accommodation. Abdullah drove me to the only 'Hoteli' in the main street, the 'Angoni Arms' – better known by anyone who had stayed there as the Agony Arms with good reason. He then drove the truck to the Boma vehicle compound where it would be secure for the night. Everyone had been told to be ready for a 7:30 a.m. start in the morning but we would have to sort out the suspension before continuing our journey to Kirondatal. The Hoteli was Asian owned and consisted of a Bar / Dining Room, two bedrooms and a wash basin and toilet in the passageway. The toilet door was marked "Lavatrine" and lent itself fairly well to the various expectations of the mixed clientele likely to use it. Inside was a large wooden box with a hole cut in the top by way of a toilet seat. The box itself was hinged down one side so that it could be swung away from the wall revealing the conventional 'Squat' facilities favoured by those who consider sitting on a seat that others had used as an abomination. The family of large cockroaches living inside the box seemed content whichever mode was brought into operation. Having deposited my safari gear in one of the bedrooms and checked the facilities; a single iron bed which had clearly seen some action judging by the hammock shaped mattress. There was a mosquito net with plenty of small blood stains showing where former occupants had managed to kill mosquitoes which had managed to get under the net. There was also a small bedside table on which was an oil lamp and a box of matches and a small barred window high up on one wall. After a wash, there was no shower, I handed in my gun to the owner, Ali Hussien, and was able to get the ice cold Tusker beer I had been looking forward to for the last three hours. Ali was chatting to someone at the bar who, judging from his accent, I took to be a South African. They were discussing the problem of lions raiding the town at night and the fact that most of the local people, the Warangi, firmly believed the problem was caused by 'Lion Men'.

Singida, and the local tribes the Warangi and the Wasandawe, which overlap in Singida, gained some notoriety as a consequence of the Lion Men Trials in which people were accused of committing murders which some claimed were done by Lion Men. There has long been serious hostility between the two tribes who are riddled with superstition and are much influenced by witch doctors. (Wachawi) Women are well known to play some part as Witches involved in ritual killings some of whom have been convicted and hanged as a consequence.

The general view amongst Africans in this part of the Province, even in northern Ugogo, seems to be that lion men are kept secretly by witch doctors and are used to kill or injure people or cattle in the settling of local disputes. The mythology is that lion men are chosen because they are mentally retarded and that they are sedated or enraged by drugs administered by the witch doctors who control them. The damage they inflict on people is instigated by people wishing to harm their neighbours and they would pay for the use of lion men accordingly. African opinion presents all kinds of exotic possibilities, the commonest being that the creatures are half man half lion, that they are trained by witch doctors who cut their leg sinews so that they walk on all fours. They are also supposed to have their fingers broken and reset in the form of claws and that, when they are in action they wear lion skins. There seems to be no limit to these speculations but what is clear is that there is genuine fear of lion men amongst the local tribes. I had discussed this in the past with Maloda who was convinced that lions raiding into the township would be lion men. A more rational explanation for the behaviour of lions was the fact that the rains had failed and the game on which lions normally feed would have left the area in search of new grazing. Lions, being territorial, would be starving and hunger would drive then to look for prey on the outskirts of the township.

As Ali was leaving the bar to sort out our evening meal the South African invited me to join him in a drink and asked how far I had come.

'Thanks, I have just driven up from Itigi but have been held up on the road because of broken suspension.'

'Its only to be expected on that road – I don't think I have seen a grader between here and Manyoni in the last twelve months and the road is now worse than its ever been.'

At this point two Somalis entered the bar and asked to speak to the South African about some private business; all three of them left to carry on their discussion outside He appeared to be a typical Africaner, about six feet four, weighing about 17 stone – most of it round the waist – short cropped blond hair and wearing desert boots, a scruffy pair of khaki shorts and a well worn khaki bush jacket. I thought he might be somewhere between forty to fifty years old, but it was difficult to judge. He returned after a few minutes without explanation and I was able to offer him a drink. He asked

'What brings you to Singida?'

'Oh, I have a meeting with the District Officer in the morning and I hope to go on to Kirondatal.'

'That's an even worse road, half the time you don't know if your still on the road or in the bush. What are you travelling in?'

'A Ford truck which has seen better days but still manages to get me around.'

'Itigi is not much of a place are you based there?'

'No, just some business there but I've come up from Dodoma. Would I be right in assuming that you are South African?'

'Dead right, Jo'burg, but I've been in E. Africa for some years – still miss the old Castle Beer though.'

'Are you staying in Singida long?'

'I don't plan to but I must get the suspension fixed on my truck or I'm not going anywhere.'

Since he offered no information regarding his own presence, but seemed keen to find out my business, I thought it time to reverse the process. I had a feeling that there was something shifty about him but couldn't put a finger on it. I knew from discussions in the Provincial Security Committee meetings that Singida was regarded as an important link in the diamond smuggling chain and that local Asian traders were suspects in the smuggling operations. The diamond mine at Shinyanga, about 60 or 70 miles to the north west,was the target for smugglers and African workers at the mine still managed to get stones out despite the extensive security system. With this in mind I thought I might open him up a bit. 'What may I ask brings you to Singida or are you based here?'

He didn't like this and after some hesitation said he was down from Mbulu where he claimed he was doing inspections. Knowing that there was very little to occupy any one on inspections in Mbulu I pressed him a bit further.

'I was just wondering what kind of inspections you might do in a God forsaken place like Mbulu?' His reply astonished me although I tried not to show it.

'Well, I'm the Labour Officer and I try to carry out inspections in the northern part of the Province about every three months.'

I switched the talk to the lion problem since he had been saying earlier that people were so afraid that they were sleeping on their roofs. I said that I had better go along to see if my driver would be sleeping in the truck. Wondering how best to handle this I walked along to the Police post at the bottom of the main street thinking it wise to get the Police involved if only as witnesses. It struck me that there may be some connection with the diamond smuggling problem bearing in mind the discussions between South African and the two Somalis earlier on. It was just possible that the local Police may have their own information about this character and a good start would be to consult them as a first step. The Sergeant in charge of the Police Post was an alert Mchaga. A tribe well known for being better educated and generally much brighter than the average African in this part of the world. Having explained the fact that I had encountered an imposter claiming to be a Labour Officer and describing the individual in some detail I asked if anything was known about him. The Sergeant explained that the CID Officer was attending a Court case in Manyoni but he was pretty sure that, as far as this person was concerned, nothing was known, otherwise they would already be keeping an eye on him.

I mentioned his connection with the two Somalis and wondered whether there might be some link with the diamond smuggling problem. With this in mind the Sergeant broke into a huge grin and clearly couldn't wait to go along and put him under arrest. I had to point out that the only evidence we had was my own statement and it would be better if we could get him to make his claim to be a Labour Officer in the hearing of other witnesses.

We decided that he and an Askari should come back to the Hoteli with me and wait outside the bar, but within hearing distance, until I called them. The Afrikaner was still in the bar when I returned and he had taken care of a few more bottles of Tusker in my absence. By this time there were four or five other customers in the bar, Asians and Africans, as well as Ali who was watching things very carefully from the other side of the counter.

'Hello, I could have done with your services as a Labour Officer in dealing with my driver who is arguing about his overnight subsistence allowance. I imagine that a lot of your work is dealing with wage claims as workers seem to get more 'bolshie' every day?'

'Its no problem for me mate, once I've had a word with the employer I soon sort them out. They are usually telling a pack of lies and if there is any nonsense I just fill em in.'

'You know I think you have some explaining to do.'

'Oh, why is that?' I called the Sergeant and the Askari in and said, 'Sergeant, would you tell this man who I am?'

'Yes Sir, you are the Labour Officer.' Turning to the Afrikaner I said, 'Would you explain in front of these witnesses why you are impersonating a Labour Officer?' He then glared at me for a few seconds and I thought for a moment I was due for a battering but he finally lent over the bar with his head in his hands muttering 'Bloody Hell'. I said 'I think it would be better if we sorted this out at the Police Post don't you?' With the Sergeant and Askari either side he walked with us to the Police Post. Once inside he asked to speak to the CID Officer and was told he wasn't available.

'I can very quickly sort this out' and fishing about in the pockets of his safari jacket he finally produced a Warrant Card which he passed to me for examination. This showed that he was a Stock Theft Prevention Officer based in the Northern Province and by way of explanation said he was carrying out an undercover operation tracing stolen cattle from over the Kenya border. This would certainly explain the presence of Somali cattle traders who were supplying him with information.

'Why on earth did you think you could get away with pretending to be a Labour Officer?'

'I understood that Labour Officers very seldom got this far north of the Province and that has been my experience till now.'

'Why didn't you liaise with the local Police since you are miles out of your own District?'

'The CID Officer knows all about me and I would have been in touch with him as soon as I have something useful to report.'

'Well, you have certainly blown your cover so far as Singida is concerned, assuming that Ali Hussian and the people in the bar don't already know about you, but that is something you will have to sort out yourself.'

'Its worse than that mate, I know that Hussian is up to his neck in the stock theft operation but my chances of nailing him now are completely scuppered.'

The next morning we drove the truck into the only garage in the township which was owned by a Lebanese who had a number of commercial interests in the District. The problem with the rear suspension was self evident, a broken leaf spring and the question was did they have a new one. I left Aron to keep an eye on this and went off to the Boma to sign the District Book. On my arrival the District Commissioner was holding a meeting in his office and asked me to join him. He was speaking to a Local Chief and three Sub-Chiefs and was obviously pretty angry about the way these people had been behaving. It soon became apparent that the main issue was the failure of the Local Authority to collect Poll-Tax and the delays which had occurred in getting people to prepare their shambas for the short rains which were now due. These problems were almost a permanent feature in most Districts of the Province but it seemed to be compounded in Singida by the surliness and lack of interest in the people concerned. The D.C. really tore into them and finished the meeting by setting targets for the collection of tax with a deadline of two months and threatened them with the ultimate sanction of

dismissal if the targets were not met. Judging by the attitude of
the Chiefs as they filed out there seemed to be no grounds for
optimism and the problem with the threat of dismissal would be
the D.Cs. loss of credibility if he failed to secure the Provincial
Commissioner's agreement to such dismissals.

In the course of a more general discussion I alerted him to the
problem of the Stock Theft Prevention Officer at which he
complained that he was fed up with lunatics coming into his
District un-announced and causing chaos. So far as the
Kirondatal problem was concerned he said that the Water
Development Engineer had passed through on his way to Dodoma
leaving a Works Superintendent in charge of the dam project. It
was his understanding that work had stopped and whatever
labour problems there were remained unresolved. The D.C. was
just completing a three year tour in Singida and seemed to be
showing all the signs that he was certainly overdue for long leave.
I assured him that I would get up there as soon as the truck was
fixed and that I would keep him informed of developments on my
way back. I found little progress when I returned to the Garage
because there was no spare leaf spring available and it was
thought that the only solution was to get a message to Arusha
some 120 miles further north over bad roads. The Arusha
proposal would probably mean a three day delay and there could
be no guarantee that a suitable spring would be available even
then. Since there was no spare vehicle to be had in Singida it was
obvious that some other solution would have to be found.

In discussions with Kikides, the Lebanese garage owner, it was
mentioned that a local duka wallah had an old 5 ton truck which
was being broken for scrap and it might be possible to get a leaf
spring off that but it would be the wrong size. In the event this is
what we had to do and getting the spring off the truck was not
difficult but cutting a leaf spring to correct size would certainly be
a real problem. The spring was made of hard tempered steel and
neither a hacksaw nor a chisel would make any impression on it.
Since no one seemed to have any idea as to how this might be
tackled it was interesting to see the teams reaction as I made a big
charcoal fire. I fanned it up to a bright cherry red heat then

placed the leaf spring in the heart of the fire until it too was bright red hot. I then pulled it out and buried it in loose soft dry sand and as it cooled the temper would be softened to the point where the metal would be workable. When it was cool enough to work on we were able to cut the spring to the right length although we broke two hacksaw blades for which Kikides charged us. Now the spring had to be re-hardened and tempered again. The process of getting the charcoal fire back up to bright red and the spring up to cherry red heat again was watched with great interest by Maloda and company who were convinced that I was performing some kind of witch craft. They were especially interested when I slowly lowered the red hot spring into a dhebi of cold water – the rate of cooling was critical, too fast and the metal would be brittle and would easily crack, too slow and the temper would be lost and the spring become useless. The team watched this intently as blacksmiths in the Wagogo tribe carry out their business of making iron implements, knives, spears, pangas etc. in secrecy and are greatly valued, even revered. I don't think this performance did much harm to whatever reputation I might have had with the messengers. Abdullah on the other hand seemed to view the whole operation with some scepticism.

It was early afternoon when we left Singida and I had warned the team to get some food to take with us as there would be little chance of getting anything in Kirondatal. The suspension on the truck seemed to be holding up quite well considering the poor condition of the road. Grey clouds were building up to the north and since we were driving in that direction rain before sunset seemed a possibility. In anticipation of this, in some of the shambas as we passed near the road, women were busy preparing the ground ready for planting. About 20 miles out of Singida we ran into what seemed at a distance to be a snow storm until Aron explained that what we were seeing was a cloud of dudus (insects). When we reached them they turned out to be small white butterflies, hundreds of thousands of them flying east to west across the road. At one point the cloud was so dense that Abdullah had to switch on the windscreen wipers to see where we were going.

Kirondatal turned out to be little more than a village of mud and wattle huts most in poor condition but there were two or three Asian owned dukas in the main street. Aron made enquiries as to the whereabouts of the dam site and we drove off in the direction indicated although it wasn't much of a road, more like a narrow track through the bush. Eventually the bush opened up into savanna type country and in the distance we could see an aluminium caravan of the type used by the Geological Surveys Department. As we approached a man emerged from the van who looked like a Goan and in fact turned out to be the Works Superintendent. He set about explaining the situation which so far as the labour dispute was concerned seemed pretty messy. Work had stopped completely and the labour force had mainly dispersed although there were some people occupying grass bandas which were in use as temporary accommodation. We then had a look at the construction site which was designed to provide three earth work dams in cascade fashion running across a slight valley much of which had been cleared of vegetation. Given reasonable rainfall the water would flow down the valley into the first dam and then flow through an overspill into a second dam, sited lower down the valley, and then through a further overspill into the last dam. The first dam was almost completed and the second had reached the halfway stage when the dispute started and work stopped.

The problem centred round the non-payment of wages, which were long overdue, and a further problem had arisen over the work tasks which workers claimed had been set too high. The real problem was that the Water Development Department had assigned the labour component of the construction contract to a Sub-Contractor who was responsible for recruiting the workers, setting their tasks and paying their wages. It soon became apparent that the Superintendent was fed up with the whole business due in part to the intransigence of the work force, the poor supervision of the Sub-Contractor and the isolation. He was also upset because in the survey and layout stage, the level pegs had been removed and the site resurveyed. I proposed that we should set up a meeting with Sub-Contractor and then a more general meeting with the workers. He didn't like this but reluctantly agreed although he felt it would be a waste of time.

Using his motor bike he set off for Kirondatal to alert the
Contractor and spread the word about the meeting set for ten
oclock the next morning. In the meantime I set about finding a
suitable site to pitch the tent for the night.

When the tent was almost assembled I was surprised to see a small
fox terrier come through the bush barking furiously followed
shortly by a European lady striding purposefully towards the
camp. She was middle aged quite smartly dressed and with an air
of authority. I walked across to greet her wondering how on earth
she happened to be in such a remote spot.

'Good afternoon.'

'What are you doing putting up that tent?'

'My name is Glynn, I'm the Provincial Labour Officer, here to
sort out the problems at the dam project. Is the tent likely to
bother you?'

'It's completely unnecessary, I am the wife of the District
Officer and when you stay in Kirondatal you are expected to stay
with us.'

'What can I say, looking at the map I had no idea that there
might be an alternative to camping – I certainly did not realise
there was a D.O. in this area.'

'It is kind of you to invite me but I am not anxious to cause any
inconvenience and I am sure I will be alright here for the night.'

'The question of inconvenience doesn't arise, we can claim
subsistence for your stay and, in any event, I wouldn't fancy your
chances in that thing given the problems we are having with lions.'

'Well, thanks. I will just have to sort something out for my
people to see that they are taken care of.'

'We are just down the hill through the bush about a quarter of
a mile. I will expect you for tea in a quarter of an hour.' With
that she called her dog and walked back down the track out of
sight.

After some discussion with the team they thought it better to
return to Kirondatal and either sleep in the truck or use their
subsistence allowance to find accommodation in the village. The
tent was stored again and Abdullah dropped me off with my safari
kit at the D.Os. residence, I removed my rifle from the rack in

the cab and took it in with me for safe keeping. On arrival a servant came out and took my kit into what I assumed was the guest room. The D.O.'s. wife then introduced herself as Margaret and seemed to be in a better frame of mind.

'Do you mind if I keep my gun in my room?'

'No, that's fine, we don't have a gun room.'

Tea with cucumber sandwiches served on the verandah gave me an opportunity to explain that this was my first visit to Kirondatal and that I had no idea that there was a D.O. stationed here, otherwise I would have followed the usual convention and let him know I was around. Like most wives in the Colonial Service she would have looked me up in the Government Staff List which would reveal my grade, pay-scale, length of service and seniority, so she could put me into some sort of social context. In general it seemed to me that it helped matters if it turned out that I was not senior to the husband on these occasions. The D.O. had left that morning for Moshi about 140 miles away in order to get some urgent dental treatment. In a remote station such as this with no European neighbours she may have been pleased to have someone around the house in the absence of her husband. The house was of standard government pattern with usual government issue furniture but it had been made very comfortable with personal possessions and family photographs about the lounge. From these it was possible to deduce that the D.O. was a much decorated wartime RAF pilot and that they had two children a boy and a girl. I was able to take a hot bath which was an unexpected luxury and a subsequent gin and tonic on the veranda watching the sun set made a welcome contrast to the arrangements at the Agoni Arms the previous evening. In front of the veranda was a small garden and beyond that the bush stretching up to the hills in distant Mbulu. African wildlife abounded in this area and it was not unusual to have gazelle, zebra, baboon and monkeys quite close to the house and in the distance giraffe, buffalo and elephant. There was a wide range of bird life including a noisy flock of weaver birds nesting in acacia trees at the edge of the garden. The dog seemed to spend a lot of time patrolling the garden fence, barking at various game scents it could detect and ever watchful for a pair of porcupines which had burrowed under the fence to raid the vegetable garden.

One of the advantages of having visitors in remote stations such as this was the possibility that they might bring with them overseas editions of English newspapers or, at second best but still welcome, copies of the Tanganyika Standard published in Dar es Salaam. Regrettably I had neither and the only paper back I carried was Evelyn Waugh's 'Black Mischief' a copy of which was already in the house. When I knew before hand that I would be staying with the local D.O. I would try to take a bottle of South African wine or, better still from the wife's viewpoint some English manufactured washing powder – Rinso was always welcome. Also if it was possible to shoot duck or guinea-fowl on the way up these too would be very acceptable. Alas, I had none of these things and so far as news was concerned I could only relate the local gossip about people we knew in Dodoma. It was dark by 6.30 and the house-boy called us to dinner; soup, roast meat (sheep or goat) and a 'shape' for dessert. The later was a set piece produced by most Swahili cooks – some form of blancmange made in a jelly mold hence the name. Whist we were drinking coffee there was a sudden crash out in the trees by the garden fence but it was too dark to see what had caused it. We had been talking about the difficulties of children's education in E. Africa and it was obvious that Margaret was really missing her own at separate boarding schools in England. My own were too young for this to be a problem but it would face us soon enough and the constant worry this would bring. It was always questionable whether the loss of children at such a formative age can ever be justified in the long term and this was a topic discussed endlessly in the Service but never satisfactorily resolved since there was no easy solution. About nine oclock, when the servants had finished their work and came in to say goodnight, the house was made secure with doors and windows locked. It was noted that the dog was absent but apparently this was not unusual and it was agreed that I would let it in when eventually it came scratching on the veranda door. Having said good night I was soon asleep In cool sheets under a clean mosquito net.

A NIGHT INTRUDER

I was awakened at about four oclock in the morning by a piercing scream from somewhere in the front of the house. After a nonsense scrambling out of the net, I ran in the dark into the lounge to find Margaret with a torch by the veranda door screaming 'there's a man in the house'. Looking round I could see a form crouched down behind the settee and having grabbed it found that it was an African, who from the smell of pombe on his breath, had had a fair amount to drink. In the struggle that followed I tried to pin his arms thinking that he might have a knife but after we crashed to the floor I was easily able to hold him down without too much trouble. While this was going on Margaret had brought my gun from my room (unloaded fortunately) and showed every sign of wanting to use it. Shining her torch on the intruder she let out another cry as she recognised him as a cook she had dismissed for insolence and thieving some weeks earlier. I took the gun from her and once the man had seen it he lay still with his hands on his head as ordered. I asked Margaret to light the Tilley lamp so that we could see what we were doing and to call her servants from the quarters behind the house. Until now the man hadn't said a word but now with the gun pointing at him and sensing that I was very angry started to sob 'Usipiga bunduki bwana,pole sana' – don't fire the gun sir I'm very sorry'. It turned out that Margaret had heard some noise in the night and thinking it was the dog had got up to let it in.

It was obvious that Margaret had had a really frightening experience and now the drama was over she was beginning to come to terms with what had happened. When the servants appeared I told them to make some tea as quickly as possible and eventually with a cup of hot sweet tea in her hand we were able to discuss how best to handle the situation. Since there was a Police Post in Kirondatal I thought I might take him down there and get him locked up pending formal charges. By now Margaret was beginning to think about what might have happened had she been alone and she made it clear that she did not want to be left alone in any circumstances. I could well understand this and we finally decided to lock the intruder in the store and at first light send the House-boy, who owned a bicycle, to take a note to the police requesting that an Askari be sent out immediately to make an arrest. I then tried to persuade Margaret to return to bed and try to get some sleep but she would not have this and started to worry about the dog which thus far had failed to return. This was beginning to look like a double tragedy as she was deeply attached to the dog, which was her constant companion, and bearing in mind the crash we had heard at sunset, I feared the dog may have been taken by a leopard. Should this prove to be the case there was every possibility that Margaret would be inconsolable. What she really needed was her husband or failing that some contact with a friendly European such as the D.Os. wife in Singida. With this in mind I sent Abdullah with a note to the D.O. in Singida as soon as he reported in the morning.

The long term consequences of an event like this were really quite serious if, understandably, the D.O. would hence forth be reluctant to leave his wife alone when he had to be on safari and the confidence of his wife, having been so badly shaken, would be unlikely to be restored if she had to endure regular periods of isolation. These were problems which the Colonial Service had to face from time to time and solutions such as postings to less remote stations did not always resolve such matters satisfactorily. Early next morning an armed police corporal handcuffed the offender and took him off to Kirondatal. There was still no sign of the dog and I could see no trace of it as I searched the bush round the bottom of the garden. When I mentioned this to the House-boy he commented 'shauri ya chui bwana' a problem with a leopard sir, which only confirmed my own suspicions. When the team arrived with the truck I sent Abdullah off to Singida with a note. I explained the situation to Aron and introduced him to Margaret suggesting that he remain with her to keep an eye on things until I returned from the meeting which had been set up with the workers at the dam. She was obviously still upset but

Frank Glynn

quietly agreed to this arrangement until I could get back. Aron was very good at dealing with Memsahibs upset by domestic difficulties and servants and his tact and sensitivity would certainly be welcome in this situation. I asked the messengers to look for any trace of the dog but nothing was found.

SETTLING A STRIKE

My worst fears were confirmed when we reached the dam site just before 10 oclock. Instead of 50 or 60 workers who should have been there, a crowd in excess of a hundred had already gathered and more people were arriving as time went on. It turned out that the Works Superintendent had passed the word in the village that there was to be a 'Baraza' at the dam site which gave entirely the wrong signal. A Baraza is a meeting of all the people in the area, usually called by the District Officer, to make announcements on development or tribal issues at which Sub-chiefs and Headmen are expected to attend as well as the local population. Topics usually considered included such things as tax collection, stock theft, agricultural and conservation issues, tribal boundaries and grazing problems, land disputes and prices for agricultural products. The objective was to present people with information and provide them with an opportunity to set out their own views on whatever subject came up for discussion. Attempts to explain that I was only concerned with labour problems connected with the dam construction got nowhere – the people had come and they were going to have their say regardless.

This meant sitting in the hot sun, there wasn't a vestige of shade, listening to the Wasandawe elders ventilating their favorite topic regardless of time. So far as the dam was concerned this was only mentioned in two context:-
    'Why should we lose all this valuable grazing land just because strangers want to put a dam here?' In reality the whole valley was scrub-land and blowing sand.
    'What are we going to do with our women who will cause trouble because they will have nothing to do?' The women currently had to carry water by head loads over a journey of about 4 miles twice a day but tribal custom forbade them to speak.
    By mid day, when it was really hot, most of the people had lost

Frank Glynn

interest and drifted away, the only people who remained were the workers who, rightly it turned out, had not been properly paid. It took a fair amount of time with the Works Superintendent and the Sub-Contractor, checking the Pay Roll and the Kipandis to determine who had not been paid and how much was owed. It was a common practice in projects where there was a deadline to be met, e.g. tobacco, coffee or pyrethrum harvesting, for workers to be persuaded to continue working on a second kipandi at a higher rate of pay so as to guarantee a stable labour force during the harvesting season. In this case it was intended to keep the work force together so as to complete the dam before the rains came. A kipandi is a monthly work ticket with 30 spaces on it, each space being marked at the completion of a days work or the set work task. Each kipandi showed the workers name, the daily rate of pay and his thumb print to identify him. When a kipandi was completed payment was due immediately and extending the period of service without pay was illegal.

Regarding the question of work tasks, it became clear from an examination of the actual job carried out by the daily paid workers that there was a real problem. There was a difference between the work on one side of the valley compared with the same task on the other side due to a change in the geology. On one side the ground was hard laterite rubble and stones, while on the other side it was mostly soft sand with the consequence that workers shovelling sand could complete their task in 4 or 5 hours, those digging laterite would take at least 6 hours to move the same amount of earth. The fact that this simple problem had not been spotted by the Sub-Contractor or the Works Superintendent indicated the poor level of supervision accorded to the work. The problem was easily resolved by adjusting the tasks to take account of the difference in work load due to variations in soil. Regarding the unpaid wages, although the amount outstanding was agreed with the Sub-Contractor it was evident that he did not have the money to pay. It also transpired that he was working for Kikides, the Lebanese trader in Singida who had negotiated the contract with the Water Development Department in Dodoma. I decided that we would all go to Singida, to make sure that the money was paid to the Sub-

Contractor who would then return to the dam and, with the Works Superintendent as witness, pay out the labour force. Before leaving for Singida I called at the house to see how Margaret was coping to find that her husband the D.O. had returned and he had everything under control but it was evident that he was a very worried man and understandably angry at the turn of events. The dog incidentally was never seen again. In Singida, Kikides first denied all responsibility for the labour situation at the dam but under pressure finally admitted his involvement and claimed that he was unable to pay until he had a subvention from the Water Development Department. This was just a smoke screen which was demolished when I threatened immediate prosecution under the Employment Act. Reluctantly he found the money and this was paid to the Sub-Contractor, in my presence and with the Works Superintendent as witness, then they both returned to Kirondatal to make payment to the workforce.

Having briefed the D.C. Singida of the outcome of my visit to Kirondatal we then faced the long hot dusty journey back to Dodoma via Itigi where I was surprised to find that work on re-building the Latrine Block was almost complete except for fitting the roof sheets. During our journey home I was discussing the outcome of our visit to the dam with Aron when he explained the reason why the survey pegs had been removed at the completion of the levelling process. It was a well understood practice amongst the Wagogo and the Warangi and possibly the Wasandawe that if you planned to put a spell on your neighbour you placed signs, sticks or piles of stones, around the boundary of his shamba. The Wasandawe would be quick to spot the survey pegs being driven in to the ground for no apparent reason and their secret removal would be seen as the best way to protect themselves.

On the return journey we stopped at a duka in Manyoni and while we were drinking Fanta orange the team were discussing the break-in at the D.Os. house at Kirondatal. The consensus was that the man must have been 'Lewa' -drunk, however Maloda closed the discussion with the comment that 'Bwana Robson-

Gibson would have shot his ass off'. It became clear that, not withstanding my performance annealing, hardening and tempering a red hot broken spring, I still had some distance to go if I was to get in the same league as my predecesser.

PART 5

THE INDIAN CINEMA

It started when I was doing a store check with Panjawani and we came across a Remington typewriter with a wide scale platen and which seemed to be in reasonable condition. Panjawani explained that it didn't work properly and was earmarked to be sold when the next Government surplus auction was organised. From its appearance it seemed to be in much better condition than the one Mr. Johnathan was using which was prone to jammed keys and had an uncertain carriage return mechanism. It also had a much better typeface but, according to Panjawani, the main problem was the ribbon feed and a failed carriage return function. It seemed that there was no typewriter 'fundi' in Dodoma who might repair it or in the Central Province for that matter. So on an impulse I told Abdullah the driver to take it up to my house with a view to my having a good look at it when time permitted. In the event after stripping it down and cleaning and oiling it, I was able to rectify the faults by adjusting the carriage return spring and unclogging the ribbon feed by straightening out the rim of the tape ribbon spool. Johnathan was delighted with result and the switch of machines substantially improved the appearance of the Department's correspondence.

Panjawani had taken careful note of this development and it wasn't long before he raised the problem of his broken radio set and asked if I might repair it. Apparently he had spent quite a lot of money on this and was really upset that it had now failed to work so I half promised to have a look at it sometime but no definite arrangement was made. However, that same evening a car drove into my drive in which was Panjawani and a large Indian manufactured heterodyne radio with an impressive wave band tuner.

It took Panjawani and the driver to carry the thing into the house where it was placed on a coffee table in the lounge. Asked what was wrong with it he looked surprised and simply said I don't know one minute it was working then it stopped and refuses to start again. He then promptly disappeared claiming that this was a hired car and he had to return it – clearly the problem was now mine.

After dinner I plugged the set into the mains and tried the controls but the radio seemed completely dead. My knowledge of radio was mainly theoretical and mostly related to army anti-aircraft radar equipment. However, the difference here was that in an army workshop one had access to sophisticated metering instruments and a full range of spares, here in Dodoma I would have to manage with a couple of screw drivers and a pair of pliers.

The radio itself was very impressive, not just in size but in appearance. The cabinet was highly polished laminated plywood with dual speakers and a huge tuning dial and wave band selector listing all the stations on the planet. My son Peter, destined to become a scientist from a very early age, couldn't wait for me to take the back off to see how it might be fixed. It didn't take long to remove the screws but the back had not been removed for some time and seemed to be firmly stuck in place. It took some force to prise it off but eventually it sprung loose and suddenly dozens of huge black and brown cockroaches came running out of the set on to the table and, running like lightening, spread on to the floor. The children screamed as I tried to get the cover back in place and shouted to Peter to quickly fetch the 'Bomba'. The bomba was a large pump action spray filled with insect repellent, which we used every evening to spray against mosquitoes. Joseph, who was washing up the dinner things in the kitchen, came through to the lounge to see what all the fuss was about and promptly started stamping on the cockroaches with his bare feet as they ran about the floor. Wyn, in the meantime had rushed into the kitchen to fetch a sweeping brush and shovel Not withstanding a good dousing with the bomba it took some time for the insecticide to work on the cockroaches although it did slow them up a bit but it took about ten minutes to account for them all. Some had got under the furniture and others had managed to get into the passage leading to the kitchen and bedroom unit.

Apart from the sudden shock of the cockroaches appearing the size of them was even more surprising, some were almost three inches in length and as Joseph trod on them on the polished floor they made a sickeningly loud squelching noise which was equally revolting. As soon as I could I carried the radio out on to the veranda where it was given some more punishing treatment with the bomba and left overnight. Wyn was concerned that someone might steal it to which I could only reply that I would be delighted. The next time I had an opportunity to look at radio I had first to dig out all the corpses of the remaining cockroaches from inside the set before I could really examine it. There was clear evidence that the roaches had been eating much of the insulation off the internal components particularly the transformer, coils and some of the wiring. Further examination revealed that the power-input cable had been eaten bare and that the two bare wires had come in to contact causing an internal short, which blew the fuse inside the set. Fortunately, the power valves and other components were still serviceable so after protecting the wires with insulating tape and replacing fuse the power was restored and the radio worked normally. When I told Panjawani that his radio was now working again he seemed astonished and then delighted but my complaints about the cockroaches made no impression on him whatsoever; roaches in his view were simply a fact of life and certainly nothing to worry about . After he had taken it home, connected it to the aerial and found it working, Panjawani then opened negotiations as to how much I proposed to charge him for the repair. Knowing how modest was his salary and the size of his family and the fact that he was a member of my staff there could be no question of payment. However, I did extract an assurance from him that he would not put it about that I was able to repair radios. The very last thing I needed was a string of people coming to seek my help with radios, and other electrical problems.

Two weeks after the radio problem had settled down two elderly Asians came to the Department seeking an appointment with me and, thinking it was probably a labour problem, I referred them to Aron, the Labour Inspector, who would be able to help them. At this there was much shaking of heads and muttering in

Hindustani as it became clear that their business was with me and did not involve a labour problem. With the pair of them sitting comfortably in my office I called in Panjawani to help since it was evident that their English was very limited indeed. Panjawani came in looking rather sheepish and after a brief exchange with his compatriots he said, 'Sir, these people are the joint owners of the local cinema which specialises in Indian films.'

'Yes, well how can I help them?'

'Well, Sir, the projector at the cinema has broken down and they have not been able to show films for weeks.'

'Really, I hadn't heard about this and I am sorry but I don't understand how something like this might involve the Labour Department. Ask them why have they come here?'

After a certain amount of discussion in Hindustani the younger of the two said that they had heard that I was a 'fundi' at repairing electrical equipment and they hoped that they could ask me to help them.

'Mr. Panjawani will you ask them how they had come to hear that I was a 'fundi'?'

By now Panjawani was seriously embarrassed and by rights should have been blushing but with his dark skin it was difficult to detect. Having put the question or something like it to the Asians one of them replied that 'This was the 'Habari' (news) their wives had picked up at the Temple – You know Bwana wives seem to know everything.'

This reply came so quickly that it was obviously well rehearsed and was designed to save Panjawani's face as much as anything.

'I see, can you tell me who would normally repair the projector, it must have broken down in the past and someone must have repaired it.'

'Well, we can usually get a Sikh from Dar es Salaam but he is away in Mombasa and we can not contact him.'

'But why do you think I would want to try to repair it, I have no experience of projectors and might easily cause more damage?'

'We thought you would help us because the people have nowhere to go now the cinema is closed and the women especially really miss it.' There was no mention of the admission charges which doubtless were also missed.

'Mr. Panjawani what do you think I should do?'

'Perhaps you could have a look at it, Sir, because it would really be a help to our community if you could fix it.'

'Gentlemen, I will think about this but I must first have a word with Mr. Panjawani and he will then let you know what I have decided.'

At this point Panjawani was looking decidedly shifty and after the Asians withdrew, after many Salaams and good wishes, he made a bee-line for his office until I called him back.

'I thought we had an agreement between us that you would not let people know that I had repaired your radio.'

'That's right Sir, but I haven't told anyone.'

'Then how do you explain the visitors I have just had and their request for my help?'

'It could easily be like they say that people are talking at the Temple, even my children who were really pleased to have the radio repaired, it is hard to keep a secret in my community.'

'I am sure that you must know that I am very disappointed about this. I am far too busy with my language and law exams coming up soon I need all the spare time I can get without running about trying to fix projectors. It will be refrigerators next and there will be no end to it.'

'I'm sorry about the way this has turned out but sometimes it may be God's wish.'

There seemed to be no answer to that and little point in carrying this further but I couldn't help feeling that Panjawani wouldn't have gone against my wishes unless there was some kind of financial incentive involved. It also seemed strange that the Asians at no point suggested that they would be willing to pay for whatever help I may be willing to provide. Two days later I was walking past the Cinema having just completed an inspection of Thacker Singh's workshop with Aron. Since there was about an hour to go before the Department closed for the day I decided to have a look at the projector if only to get some idea of the nature of the problem. One of the brothers was keen to show me round and to the best of his ability tried to explain what had gone wrong.

There seemed to be no problem with the power supply as the projection lamp and mirror were working satisfactorily. A young 14 or 15 year old boy who I took to be the son who filled the role of Projectionist, explained that the film kept burning out and had to be re-spliced and would then burn out again. Having removed the outer cover and tinkered about with power off it seemed likely that the sprocket feeding the film through the lens gate wasn't working and with the film static in front of the powerful projector lamp it burned out after about three seconds. I eventually discovered that the sprocket was belt driven by the motor and the belt had broken and fallen into the bottom of the outer casing. After a lot of fumbling about I was able to recover the broken belt which was clearly beyond repair. I suggested that they should take the belt to the shoe-maker in the bazaar and get him to make another with good quality leather and a strongly sewn seam.

As I arrived at the Department the next morning the two brothers were waiting outside my office with the new belt which seemed to be the correct size and with a strong well stitched overlapping seam.

I promised to call in at lunch time to try the belt which would need careful adjusting to get the right tension to avoid slipping. In the event fitting the belt was a fairly straight forward operation and there was a tensioning adjustment which made the job simpler. After replacing the outer cover the projector was switched on, a film fed in and the drive mechanism seemed to be working satisfactorily. As I left there were many Salaams and thanks since they recognised that they were now back in business, but there was no suggestion that they would pay for my help but the brother remarked that they would be seeing Mr. Panjawani. By the time I got back to the office Panjawani was already aware that the projector had been repaired and seemed pretty pleased about such a satisfactory outcome. The thought occurred to me that he may be operating as some kind of middle man which was a bit worrying. I had warned him that there could be no question of a fee which might be interpreted as my accepting bribes at a later stage. I was particularly concerned that the Asians should not be seen to be bringing a 'Zawadi' – gift – such as a case of beer, or spirits to the Department since the Africans would be quick to put their own interpretation on such a development. Panjawani had assured me that there was no need to worry and that soon everything would be settled down.

I was reminded of this curious assurance about two weeks later when I received a very nice letter, in impeccable English, thanking me for my help in repairing the projector and formally inviting Wyn and I to a special showing of a new, much publicised, Indian film. This was a very nice gesture but it was not one that we were particularly anxious to accept. The cinema was a hot cement block building with an iron corrugated roof, concrete floor, swarming with insects and hard wooden seats. These could be pretty taxing because Indian films were very noisy and always seemed to go on forever. Perhaps in our honour the performance had been arranged for a mixed audience, it was usual for shows to be designated male of female to reflect cultural preferences. We were met on arrival by the owners with some ceremony and escorted to our seats on which unusually two cushions had been provided. We were offered a choice of coca-cola or orange drinks and a tray of sweet meats, roasted almonds, coconut slices and peanut brittle. The later could almost guarantee a sharp attack of the 'squitters' and we fought a constant battle with the children to prevent them buying this from street vendors for this reason; even so they sometimes managed to get an illicit supply through the servants. Looking at the audience it was obvious that this was a gala occasion, colourful bright Sari's and clean white dhoti's were much in evidence. The atmosphere was heavy with the powerful smell of Indian perfume – jasmine and frangipani, coconut oil air dressing and the inevitable smells of garlic and curry. Most of the wealthy Asian traders together with their extended families were present and the thought occurred to me that if the rackety old projector was likely to break down of course it would happen tonight.

The lights were dimmed, the film started and the sound turned up to maximum volume as this seemed to be the preferred mode, the language was Hindi but there were Gujarati subtitles for those who needed them. Like most Indian films it started with loud traditional dance music and a group of pretty girls in colourful dresses performing in the most exotic countryside it is possible to create within a studio. The film was billed as a drama and opened up with the girls singing and dancing their way to work which surprisingly turned out to be a grim sweat shop of a spinning factory, the girls each attending to what seemed to be extremely dangerous unfenced spinning frames. The camera focussed on the pretty young girl who, whilst diligently attending her spinning frame, managed to belt out a rollicking Asian song in a singularly high pitched voice and her colleagues on other machines happily joined in the chorus – this was the heroine. The camera then swung on to the door at the end of the factory floor which suddenly swung open to reveal a rather chubby, well oiled and heavily made up man in a sharp tropical suit who entered the shop floor managing to convey the impression that he could only be the factory owners son – this was the hero. He majestically paraded along the alley between the machines occasionally fingering the cotton reels and appraising each girl in turn and managing to create the impression that fingering the cotton reels was not his only interest. Eventually he arrived in front of the heroine when the music swelled to a crescendo. The camera came into close focus on the heroine who was now sporting a lascivious grin and then switched to the hero who was so overcome that a heart attack seemed imminent. A noisy duet then followed with occasional help from the whole factory – it was obvious that a bond had been struck.

The scene suddenly changed and without any romantic context, certainly no kissing or fondling which are forbidden in Indian films, with admirable economy we find the young heroine clutching a tiny infant to her breast. With a dramatic lowering of octaves she takes us through a sad song of unhappiness and innocence betrayed. The scene switches to the young girl still clutching the baby on the door step of the factory owners mansion. Her appeals to the hero's parents are indignantly swept aside as they secretly line up their own choice of bride for the hero. He in the meantime seems to be unaware of his recently acquired parental status and for some inexplicable reason is unable to find his lost love. Perhaps this is because his search is confined to exotic night clubs with comely vocal dancers of easy virtue, wickedly modern dance music and some pretty heavy drinking and smoking. The heroine's problems worsen when her surprised parents (where have they been for the past 9 months) throw her out into the street in disgrace against an appropriate musical background. There then follows a series of adventures in which the heroine, frequently having to defend what's left of her honour, eventually finds kindness and some kind of life amongst the poor and outcast. She is cheered up from time to time by a whole series of Chaplinesque comics in dhoti's often with much singing and dancing and a hearteningly loud musical background greatly appreciated by the audience.

Eventually (when my hopes that the film really will breakdown seem to be fizzleing out) fate contrives to bring the lovers together with impeccable timing. The hero is now on the point of sealing his marriage vows at the heart of a magnificent wedding ceremony, but with unerring accuracy he recognises his young son, now a chubby little lad, and clutches him to his breast with great emotion and a crescendo of music. Pandemonium almost beyond the range of the orchestra then ensues and eventually all is explained and forgiven and the happy couple dance off singing into the sunset; leaving behind it would seem the young son and presumably the hero's inheritance. The film ends and the lights come on and everyone heaves a sigh of relief. Empty coca-cola bottles are rolled down the sloping concrete floor under the seats to the front of the cinema, the rats which have been surreptitiously feeding on the crumbs of fallen chipatis, somosas and peanuts, scurry back to their holes. The bats which have been zooming about the screen throughout the performance in the light beam from the projector now retire as do the moths and other flying insects – but not the mosquitoes.

Old men, some of them in tears, who have been contentedly chewing betal nut throughout the performance are now free to expectorate the gory end product on to the concrete floor. We finally reach the door having remembered to thank our host and with heads ringing walk out into the quiet tropical night. In my case with the firm personal resolve never ever to repair a projector again.

INSPECTING A GOLD MINE

After completing routine inspection visits in Singida I decided to extend the safari to visit a gold mine some 60 miles to the north west. The Department's file on the mine indicated that it had not been visited for some years and that it was owned by an Italian Commandatori whose family had established the mine before the war. In addition to the mine the family owned and operated a successful mixed farm and cattle ranch. Travelling out to the mine took us through typical Central Province country, mostly flat plains of scrub with occasional Baobab trees and rocky out-crops of huge boulders which gave the impression that they had been forced up out of the ground by volcanic pressures. In fact, according to the people in the Geological Survey Department, the reverse was the case and over many years the tropical rains had washed away the ground so that formerly buried rocks were now exposed. These rocks and the caves in them were the home of troops of baboon and hyraxs and were frequently raided by leopard who would use the caves when rearing cubs. This was no longer Ugogo tribal land the resident tribe being the Warangi who viewed the caves with some suspicion claiming they were occupied by dangerous spirits.

We reached the farm over an indifferent dusty bush track spotting a good variety of bird life but without incident and the truck's suspension seeming to hold up pretty well. Sadly this was not the case with Aron – whose travel sickness was getting worse – he could scarcely travel more than 40 miles without serious vomiting and I had to keep an eye on the mileage to ensure that we stopped to give him rest about every thirty miles just to give him a break. I sometimes wondered if these attacks were brought on by dust which covered us all during any safari but there was no way we could make the cab dust proof even if the windows and ventilators were kept closed Under these conditions the heat in the cab became unbearable and, inevitably all three of us were soon perspiring me more so than Aron or Abdullah. I sometimes wondered how they felt about this although it was never discussed. For me African body odour was a sharp pungent smell which reminded me of horses with a hint of wood smoke and a trace of spice. In the case of Abdullah there was in addition a smell of cheap perfume – the sort of sickening smell of the scent available in the bazaars. Inevitably I wondered if they found my smell offensive having read somewhere that the Japanese had problems with Europeans because of the cheese in their diet. So, we sat in silence jogging along in the cab each with our own perceptions. So far as Maloda and the other messengers in the back of the truck were concerned, this would not be a problem as the wind coming through the slats in the back of the truck would carry away any smell. For them there was much ribaldry about flatulence and Saidi was said to be the worst offender which he didn't seem to mind, indeed he accepted all these coarse remarks with a wide grin.

We were travelling through game country but there was not much to be seen other than a group of 9 or 10 giraffes in the far distance and there was evidence of elephants from the dung on the track. Baboons would chase across the track in front of the truck and would stop at the side of the road to watch us go past when they felt that they were safe. There was plenty of bird life including dense flocks of quaila–quaila birds and the occasional hornbill and the bush seemed ideal country for guinea fowl but none were spotted. Eventually we moved into more open savannah country and came across a magnificent Palatio, built of grey stone with an elaborate roof of red Mangalore tiles. The building stood well back from the road on a slight rise and the approach was up a long well kept gravel drive flanked on each side with a row of flame trees which provided a long strip of spectacular colour in sharp contrast to the surrounding bush. The building would not have looked out of place on the edge of the Mediterranean or Lake Como particularly as there was a well kept lawn in front of the house which was flanked on each side with orange, lemon, and paw-paw trees. As the truck came to a halt in front of the main entrance a pair of large pure bred Ridge Backs came slowly down the veranda steps, silent but with ridge of hair on their necks and shoulders fully raised indicating that they were not pleased. These dogs are specially bred for hunting lions and need to be taken very seriously. We all sat tight in the truck, no one in his right mind would take a chance with these dogs so we just sat there, unmoving. After a while I wondered if I should sound the horn, however, the door opened and an African servant wearing a red fez, white kanzu and a red waist band came towards us. He invited me into the house with a smile saying, 'Jambo, Bwana karibuni mbwa yake siyo kali' – come in the dogs are not fierce.

I cautiously left the truck and entered the hall way which was furnished on a luxurious scale with ultra modern furniture made of chrome steel and black leather and with a black and white tiled floor, partly covered with zebra skins. The servant having closed the door shutting the dogs out left me there and went off, presumably to report my presence.

A smartly dressed middle aged lady came to greet me and, after I had introduced myself, she said my husband will be glad to see you he is in the farm office. She then asked if I would like some refreshment or if I would like to see the Commandatori and then come back with him for tea. I suggested that it might be better if I let him know that I was here but that I would be grateful for some tea in due course. As I moved back to the truck the dogs followed me and it was with some relief that I got back into the cab. Driving past the front of the house we came into the track leading to the farm buildings, a collection of well designed modern buildings, barns and stores, built with burnt brick with corrugated steel roofs. As we approached the smaller of these a black Labrador dog emerged followed by an elderly white haired man, leaning heavily on an aluminium stick. He was smartly dressed in a light tropical suite with a special air of authority which suggested that he could only be the Commandatorri Having introduced myself as the Provincial Labour Officer he said, with something of a twinkle in his eye.

'We are greatly honoured, so far out in the bush we don't often get Government officials coming to inspect us so I, or my sons, will be happy to show you whatever you might wish to see. You must of course be our guest for the night but first let us go up to the house to see if we can find some tea.'

'Thank you, I should be grateful to spend the night but I must make some arrangement with my staff who are in the truck.'

'Don't worry, my Head-Man will see that they are properly taken care of so they will have nothing to worry about.'

I explained to Aron the arrangements and asked him to let me know if there were any problems. Since they all had their overnight's subsistence allowance they should be alright so we arranged to meet at 7.30 in the morning to start the inspection. I told Abdullah to take my things and the gun back to the house and said I would meet him with the others in the morning.

As the Commandatori and I walked slowly back to the house we found Abdullah sitting in the truck outside the door petrified by the Ridge-backs which were circling round the truck. The servants would doubtless have spotted his presence but since he was from a different tribe they would be enjoying his discomfort. The Commandatori promptly set about the dogs with his stick, it was a feeble effort and the dogs knew it but they finally settled down on the veranda like a pair of sentries. Tea was served in the lounge, a choice of Darjeeling, Lap Sang, or Earl Grey, with delicious cucumber sandwiches of fresh bread, an impressive looking gateaux and a variety of biscuits.- the later mostly eaten by the Labrador after much begging. We were joined by the Commandotori's wife issuing a string of orders to the two servants dispensing the tea and complaining about the presence of the dog. A complaint which the Comandotori and the dog cheerfully ignored.

'Mr. Glynn, I wonder what exactly you have come to inspect, I don't recall having had a formal inspection before, but of course we have had social calls by the Provincial Commissioner from time to time. I think the later point was to alert me to the fact that he was well connected at the highest official level.

'Well Sir, my Department is mainly responsible for ensuring that employing concerns, including mines and factories, comply with the prescribed conditions covering safety, health and welfare laid down in Labour legislation.

'I see, would I be right in assuming that you will wish to see our wages records and the condition of our labour lines – but what about the mine?'

'So far as mines are concerned the emphasis is on safe working conditions, particularly where machinery is involved we would like to see that machinery is properly fenced and that safe working practices are in place in line with the provisions of the Factories Act.'

'I see, well I don't see any problems with that and my sons will be happy to show you whatever you need to see. You know, I seem to remember that quite some time ago someone from the Department of Lands and Mines called in and he had the impression that he was responsible for ensuring mine safety and lots of other things I don't recall ever seeing his report although it would be reasonable to assume that he produced one. I wonder if you might have seen it since it must cover some of the issues you have just mentioned?'

'I must confess that I have never seen it, but then I have only recently joined the Colonial Service. I agree that I would be interested in seeing such a report if only to avoid wasting people's time by going over ground which has already been inspected.'

'Would it be fair to assume that you and your colleagues in the mines department are working close together to avoid unnecessary bureaucracy?'

'I'm afraid not, sir, but perhaps it would help if I explained that the division of responsibility between my Department and the Department of Mines is that the winding gear shaft and all that happens below ground is the Mines Departments concern, whilst what happens on the surface to the extent that it can be defined as a factory process is the responsibility of my Department.'

It was quite obvious that the Commandatori was enjoying himself, his wife was smiling at me and shaking her head but perhaps knew better than to interrupt him but he hadn't finished yet and went on to say 'Mr. Glynn, this all sounds unnecessarily complicated but I sometimes wonder if there should be another kind of inspector who, having been assured by your report that I am treating my workers properly, paying them their wages etc. would then be concerned to ensure that they are working properly, not losing my tools, stealing my maize, squatting on my land and stealing my small stock, or trying to smuggle out my gold.'

I was just about to reply, rather lamely, that he would have to rely on the common law, when we were interrupted by the appearance of one of his sons, a young man in his early twenties who reported some problem with the crushing plant. The Commandatori introduced him as Mario his youngest son and after he had helped himself to tea and a huge slice of gateaux, it was agreed that this would be a good time for Mario to take me round the mine. It was something of a relief to escape the inquisition of his father and, as we drove out to the mine in an open Landrover, Mario explained that I should watch out for him since there was nothing he liked better than interrogating government officials but it was all quite harmless. I was surprised how small and simple the mining operation seemed to be. The mine shaft was only six feet in diameter and the shaft seemed to be about 50 or 60 feet deep. The winding gear was a single pulley mounted on head gear made of steel girders and at one end of the cable was a large steel bucket in the shaft and the other end was connected to a pulley driven at the other end by a pulley and diesel engine. The bucket was wound up and down the shaft to transport workers to the seam and to remove rock, soil and ore as required. The ore was then conveyed to the nearby Crushing Plant, a large open sided wooden building, in which was housed a fairly antiquated Hammer Mill driven by a steam engine and flywheel, powered by a wood burning boiler. Water was provided by a dam which filled up during the rains and was topped up by ground water pumped up by a windmill driven pump. Apart from diesel oil required for the winding gear the whole operation was self-sustaining and much of the water used in the crushing plant was carefully recycled.

Collecting gold couldn't have been simpler, crushed ore from the hammer mill was pumped in the form of a slurry over sloping screens covered in corduroy cloth and particles of gold, being heavier that the rest of the slurry, lodged in the seams of the corduroy; this was carefully washed out in the form of gold dust which was smelted and cast into ingots. This later part of the plant was built on the lines of Fort Knox, with three-foot thick granite walls, a reinforced concrete roof and a massive steel door with security hinges and complex double locks. The whole process only employed about 30 African workers working in two eight hour shifts and three ex Askari security guards armed with single barrelled shot guns. Two of the sons supervised the whole process, one on each shift, including the maintenance of the machinery. Mario then took me on a quick tour of the adjoining farm which was extensive and managed by two Somali Headmen under the general supervision of one of the Commandatori's daughters. The farm combined dairy and beef cattle, small stock and poultry and the agricultural side grew maize, millet, and sugar with fruit such as oranges, lemons, banana, paw paw and mangoes for domestic consumption. The water needed for this level of production was a problem but the land was about 5,000 feet above sea level and generally had good rains. A stream flowing from the Mbulu mountains which became a raging torrent during the rains, but dried out in the dry season, plus two dams were sufficient to service the irrigation furrows across the farm. Given reasonable rains the farm could produce a cash crop but if the rains failed the Mine provided the necessary financial stability.

It had taken many years for the farm and mine to reach this stage of development. The Commandotori had settled in Tanganyika before the second world war and discovered the mine after extensive prospecting in the Lupa District where some gold had been discovered and in the Northern Province. He married before the war and since his wife was of Scandinavian nationality in 1938 sensing that war was inevitable he transferred the land and mining titles to her name thus avoiding the property being confiscated in war time by the Custodian of Enemy Property. When Italy declared war the Commandatori being a reserve officer in the Italian Army rejoined his unit in Italy only just escaping through Nairobi airport to avoid detention. The main problem with the farm was its isolation, the nearest towns Arusha, Moshi, and Dodoma were a formidable distance north and south and because the roads were no better than they should be transport during the long and short rains could be exceptionally difficult. However, the family had built a well laid out grass landing strip and hangar in which was kept a twin engined Piper which meant that Arusha and Moshi could be reached in under an hours flying time. The sons and both daughters held pilots licences consequently Nairobi, with its shops, hotels and good medical facilities could be reached in under two hours flying time. Since the family owned a beach house and boat at Tanga they could also visit the East African coast quite easily.

The servants had placed my baggage in a very pleasant room in the guests wing of the house and my gun in the Gun Room. Mario had let me know that I would be expected in the lounge for drinks before dinner at 6.30pm so there was ample time for me to have a bath and change before then. The bedroom was beautifully furnished and there was a bathroom ensuite in which was an enormous sunken bath, carved out of black marble, and a wash basin and toilet, hot and cold water and a shower. However, when I came to use the bath there was a problem in the form of a huge hairy spider about the size of my hand which had taken up residence in the bottom of the bath. It had doubtless fallen in to the bath during the night and because of the steep highly polished sides it was impossible for it to climb out. It was far too big to disappear down the plug hole which was itself quite large. Regardless of what the conservationists may say, for me all spiders and snakes are dangerous and this is the message we have impressed on the children, particularly since Philip was stung by a scorpion. The problem now was what to do about it. I could of course use the wash basin but no way was I going to forgo the pleasure of a nice hot bath and shower after a hot dusty day so there was no question that the spider would have to go.

I could of course make a fuss and call the servants since they would doubtless be able to take care of it. However, I had not forgotten the light hearted grilling I had received from the Commandatori and bearing in mind that this was a young family, whose amusements might be fairly limited, there was a remote chance that this situation might have been contrived. But this was getting me nowhere so I looked around for something handy with which to dispatch the spider and as there was nothing suitable I would have to use one of my desert boots. As I leaned over the bath the spider was alert and could doubtless see me but a quick smart rap with heel of my shoe should do the trick. Not a bit of it, before my shoe came anywhere near it the spider shot along the bath with uncanny speed and almost reached the rim but slipped back as the polished surface defeated it. It took about five or six carefully aimed blows before I could register a hit and this only had the effect of removing two of its legs. There was a pause then as I tried to convince myself that the battle was over but the missing legs seemed to have no effect on the speed with which it was able to duck and weave. It seemed as though the spider knew precisely where my next blow would fall so new tactics were needed. I then used both my shoes, one in each hand, which seemed to put the spider right off its stroke. I had to be careful, however, it had occurred to me that the only way the spider would be able to get out of the bath was over my shoe and up my arm, it was just a matter of time before the spider worked this out too. It took nine or ten shots to bring the matter to a close and the problem then was how to dispose of the messy remains. I hated touching the thing but finally managed to wrap it in toilet paper and put it the waste paper basket in the bedroom.

Finally, after a long soak in a really hot bath and a quick cold shower I was able to change and go along to the lounge at the appointed time. All the family were present and the Commandatori, with great formality explained that I was here to inspect them and introduced his daughters, Gina and Marina, his other son Lorenzo and a young German architect Klaus. Lorenzo was almost the twin of Mario but 12 months older, the two girls were in their early twenties and very good looking, Klaus, a German architect, had been commissioned to build a bridge over the river, was about thirty years old and prone to heel clicking. All of them were formally dressed, the men wearing jackets and ties and the ladies in very smart stylish dresses. Fortunately I had changed into my only long sleeved shirt, clean slacks and a tie but no jacket. The Commandatori was in a more friendly mood and very conscious of his duties as the host offering a wide choice of drinks and enquiring about my comfort. Lorenzo asked if I had settled in nicely and if things were satisfactory in the guest wing. I replied that I was very impressed with standard of comfort saying that it was an unexpected surprise quite different to what I normally find. Mario asked if there was plenty of hot water as it sometimes it is slow to get through to the guest wing. Everyone was silent at this point and they were all waiting to see how I would reply. Conscious of the silence I replied that, 'There was only one minor problem, there was someone already in the bath before I could get in.'

'Someone' said Mario.

'Well a pretty large spider actually'

'How on earth did you manage, or did you call a servant?'

'I am afraid that I really dislike spiders, especially the huge hairy variety, and I treat them all as dangerous.'

'So, how did you manage to remove it?'

'It was something of a performance actually but I finally dispatched it with the heel of my shoe.'

'Are you saying that you have killed it ?'

'I'm afraid so I didn't fancy sharing a bath with it.'

The silence was then broken by Gina who, dead on cue, called out in the dramatic voice of a tragic actress 'Oh my poor 'Musso' he is a household pet and completely harmless' staring at me reproachfully. The rest of them where obviously quietly enjoying my discomfort but the Commandatiri's wife kindly intervened by saying

'You must not upset your self Mr. Glynn. These are very naughty children, there are plenty of spiders here, too many of them, and we certainly have none as household pets – they are just trying to tease you.'

'Oh, thank you that's a great relief, but I haven't yet disposed of the body so if Gina would like to bury it perhaps something can be arranged.'

At this everyone seemed to burst out laughing and conversation switched to more domestic matters.

Dinner was formal, elaborate and exceptionally good, served by two African servants and a wine steward. Spaghetti was the first course, followed by a fish course of talapia caught in the dam that day and served with an ice cold Frascatti. The main course was roast lamb, farm reared, and served with a very superior classic Chianti. Every one seemed to be in good form and conversation in English and Italian focussed on the best time to go fishing on the coast. After an excellent Zabaglione the Commandatori, who was fairly mellow by then, returned to the charge.

'Mr. Glynn, would I be right in assuming that you have seen some military service?'

'Yes Sir, I recently left the army to join the Colonial Service.'

'I thought so. Would I also be right in assuming that you were an officer in the Armoured Corps?'

'Actually, I was a Captain in the Royal Artillery.'

Every one at the table had settled down to listen to this interrogation presumably knowing what was to come.

'I see, did you manage to serve in the last war?'

'I was mobilised with the Territorial Army at the outbreak of war in 1939 and served throughout the war.'

'I wonder if your war service involved you in the campaigns in the Western Desert?'

'No, during war time I was in a Heavy Anti Aircraft Regiment and saw most of my action in the Battle of Britain.'

'Then Mr. Glynn I must accept that to me you are another disappointment.'

At that point he seemed to lose all interest in conversation and proposed that we should take coffee in the lounge. As we were leaving the table Mario quietly said 'Don't worry about father, he received a quite serious leg wound in North Africa and he has this conviction that sooner or later he will meet the people who shot him.' After coffee, Lorenzo, Mario and Marena suggested that we should play snooker, Gina and Klaus, who apparently were engaged to be married, went off to their own affairs.

A full size billiard table was available in one of the wings of the house and we spent the rest of the evening playing. It was soon clear that my performance was well below that of the members of the family and eventually we went off to bed.

I found myself in a nice comfortable bed inside the mosquito net and was soon soundly asleep. I woke about 1.00 am for no apparent reason, every thing was still and as quiet as the African night ever gets except that I thought I could hear a lion roaring close to the house. The Masai have it that the first long roar is the lion saying 'Whose land is this?' and that the subsequent short coughs are the reply 'Yangu, Yangu, Yangu' – mine, mine, mine. The next morning I woke to find a trail of ants coming through a gap in the window down the wall and across the floor to the waste basket in which I had left the remains of the spider. I should have anticipated this as ants have an incredible capacity for searching out food and they were now in the process of carting off small pieces of the dismembered body back to their nest. I dumped the remains in the toilet and flushed them away knowing that the ants would quickly disperse once the food had gone. After an excellent breakfast Mario asked what I would like to see so we walked down to the farm office where Aron and the team were waiting by the truck. At my suggestion we started at the farm labour lines, Mario led off in the Land Rover over well maintained farm tracks Aron following with the others in the truck. The buildings housing the farm workers were well sited and well spaced so as to reduce the fire hazard. The buildings were semi-permanent, made of burnt brick with thatched roofs each with a secure door and a concrete stance in front for cooking fires. They were occupied mostly by women and children and a few elderly people, chickens, goats and dogs were much in evidence and there was a general air of well being; most of the men and some women were at work in different parts of the farm. So far as sanitation was concerned, an adequate number of well spaced deep-pit latrines had been constructed at an appropriate distance from the housing. Aron went through his usual routine dropping stones down the pits to check whether they had filled up sufficiently to justify their being filled in and new pits constructed so as to avoid fly breeding. All the stances had wooden covers again to reduce fly breeding but only a few of these were fitted in place. Mario watched this process with some scepticism remarking that it was one thing for an employer to provide adequate sanitation but it was another matter trying to ensure that the facilities were used as intended. According to him, most of the Warangi had an abhorrence of using the same facility as others and consequently a piece of waste ground had been set aside in the nearby bush as an alternative, fly breeding and pollution notwithstanding. Close to the labour lines was a small but clean dispensary where a part time dresser was employed in the evening to deal with local medical problems. The ration store was sited at the other end of the lines and a Storeman, supervised by Gina, issued rations of maize meal, sugar, palm oil, and vegetables or fruit in season to a prescribed scale; meat was issued once a week.

The farm employed about 40 workers male and female on a kipande basis with eight drivers and fundi's paid on monthly contracts. Additional casual labour were employed in the planting and harvest seasons but were often hard to recruit because at those times people were busy with their own 'shambas'. The wages records which were kept in the farm office were well maintained and disputes over payments seldom presented problems. The wage rates were determined primarily by the rate at which people agreed to work. Unless they were offered a real incentive over what they could earn on their own shambas they wouldn't offer their labour. The wages of the employees at the mine were set on a completely different scale reflecting the skilled and semi-skilled nature of the work involved. Here the labour force was more stable some employees having worked for a good many years and they were the beneficiaries of a provident fund scheme which would take care of their retirement. Disputes over pay were fairly limited, mostly about how much a worker could claim in cases where they failed to complete the 30 day kipandi; aggrieved workers in these circumstances would disappear taking with them tools or farm property. Major disputes affecting a number of workers were rare and these were usually caused by inter-tribal or social problems unrelated to employment issues and were often resolved by resort to the local Sub-Chief or, less frequently, the witch doctor. The workshop where vehicles and tractors were maintained, and where accidents might be expected to happen, seemed to be well organised, fire extinguishers and first aid equipment were readily available, arc-welding equipment was properly earthed and drilling and other moving machinery was safely fenced. Petrol, oil and lubricants, were kept in a separate building made of permanent materials and a safe distance from all the other buildings.

All in all the farm was a model of its kind and in sharp contrast to the majority of farms I had to inspect. This doubtless reflected the fact that it was highly capitalised operation supervised by a team of young people with progressive ideas. The mining operation was another issue, partly because the machinery and prime movers were old and subject to constant use leaving little time for routine maintenance. The gaskets on the diesel engine driving the winch gear were leaking and oil was seeping down the engine casing close to the exhaust – a potential fire hazard. The belt drive to the cable winding drum was unfenced – the metal guards had been removed perhaps to carry out repairs but had not been replaced. More worrying was the fact that the safety valve on the steam boiler at the crushing plant had been tied down with a piece of rope to render it inoperative. This was serious, in effect there was nothing to stop the steam pressure in the boiler from exceeding the prescribed safe limits and exploding with disastrous consequences. There was a pressure gauge indicating the pressure level so that at least this was known and steam could be blown off by the operator before the pressure reached the danger mark on the gauge – provided that this was spotted in time. This was an obvious contravention of the Factories Act and justified closing the plant down immediately. Mario explained that Alfredo was responsible for the mine and that he would call him as he was working down at the rock face. As Aron and I waited for Alfredo to appear I asked him to find the man who normally looks after the boiler and to get him to join us, however no one could be found which suggested that the boiler was left unattended except to feed in the wood fuel and fill up the water in the boiler.

When Alfredo emerged I drew his attention to the problem and he promptly removed the rope from the safety valve from which a cloud of high pressure steam burst out indicating that the boiler was working well beyond the safety limit. There then followed a rather heated exchange in Italian between Alfredo and Mario in which the Commandatori's name was frequently mentioned. As the argument went on they seemed to be getting pretty emotional and I decided to intervene.

'Can I suggest that we go outside and discuss this calmly and sensibly, no amount of shouting is going to help matters.' Alfredo

looking far from calm replied, 'My father should be here because
this is his problem.'

'Yes alright, but before we get him involved let us first get a
proper understanding as to what is going on., why did you tie the
safety valve down in the first place?' In some exasperation
Alfredo replied 'This is a very old boiler which has seen a lot of
service with the groundnut scheme and it is under powered when
driving the Crushing Plant. To keep the plant operating
efficiently we need maximum pressure from the boiler but the
safety valve is set too low to achieve this.'

'Do you really think that the designers of the boiler who set the
safety limits would approve of your deliberately ignoring those
limits?'

'I know its an old boiler but I also know that the safety valve
is set to provide a low pressure level and within reason it can be
operated slightly above the prescribed limit.'

'But with the safety valve tied down the way I found it there
is simply nothing to stop the pressure building up to the point of
explosion, isn't that the case?'

'No, I have been working with this boiler for many years and
it has never exceeded the limit in all that time.'

'Alfredo, I don't think you understand the seriousness of what
I am saying. Let me put it this way, if the boiler explodes because
the safety valve has been deliberately rendered inoperative by
you and one of your workers is killed you would be charged by
the courts with manslaughter. Do you really believe that the
court would accept your defence that you needed a bit more
pressure?'

Alfredo was unwilling to respond to that and a further
argument in Italian started up between the two brothers which
became emotional very quickly. Finally, Alfredo said the he has
long sought to have the boiler replaced with something more
modern and highly powered but his father had failed to agree and
that's the end of it.

'It may seem to be the end of it for you but it certainly isn't the
end of it for me. As a Factory Inspector I have just come across
a dangerous piece of machinery the safety mechanism of which
has been deliberately rendered inoperative. Perhaps I should
remind you that in these circumstances I have a duty to ensure

that the dangerous machinery concerned is immediately put out of use even if it means closing down the whole process. In addition I have also to consider whether an offence has been committed under the Factories Act and whether this warrants a prosecution. My Inspector here is a witness to this discussion and his evidence together with mine should easily secure a conviction if I should decide to proceed along these lines.'

Mario, who seemed to have a better grasp of what I had been saying, then said

'Mr. Glynn I am sure that we fully understand what you are saying and we can guarantee that, henceforth, the safety valve mechanism will remain adjusted in the safe position so what do you now expect us to do?'

'What I suggest we do is that we go back to the house and let your father know about these developments as a first step. Then if you feel it would help you could have a private discussion to decide how you wish to proceed. I could then join you and we could perhaps agree on the next steps.'

They clearly didn't relish the idea of bringing the Commandatori into the discussion but could see no realistic alternative so this was agreed. Back at the house the sons and daughters were all assembled and it was apparent that Alfredo had briefed them on the problem. The Commandatori in a pretty grim mood opened the proceedings making it pretty obvious that he was very annoyed.

'Mr. Glynn I understand that you are having some difficulty in connection with the boiler, what exactly is your problem?'

'It is not my problem it is yours and put quite simply in the course of my inspection I found that the safety valve on the boiler had been deliberately interfered with so as to render it inoperative and that the boiler was under pressure at the time.'

'I understand that Alfredo has explained the reasons for this to you and I must point out that he, unlike you, has extensive experience in operating the boiler.'

'In my view there can be no justifiable reason for disabling crucial safety equipment on potentially dangerous machinery when it is in operation. I have explained to Alfredo that he has committed an offence under the Factories Act and rendered himself liable to prosecution.'

'Don't you find it rather strange that one minute you are a welcome guest in my house and the next you are threatening me with prosecution?'

'No one could be more embarrassed than I am at this moment, but I have a duty to bring this matter to your attention and, perhaps more importantly, to try and find a satisfactory way in which the problem can be rectified and the offence not repeated.'

'I see, so what exactly do you have in mind?'

'The essential first step is to ensure that the safety valve on the boiler is set so that it can efficiently carry on the job it is designed for. The second problem is to make whatever modifications may be necessary to valve equipment to ensure that it can't be tampered with again so as to render it inoperative.'

'So, Mr. Glynn, you are now an engineer and just how precisely do you propose to make these necessary modifications?'

'With the greatest respect, Sir, making the necessary changes is essentially your business, it certainly isn't mine. In any event, now that the restraints have been removed from the valve it may now be working correctly but this can easily be verified by raising the steam pressure to see if it functions at the correct pressure.'

'Alfredo, does that make sense to you?'

'Yes father, I see no problems with that.'

'Now Mr. Glynn, there is the problem of making sure that the safety valve can't be tampered with. What do you have to say about that?'

As I said earlier, this is essentially your problem but I'm sure that there is enough talent in your family to devise a satisfactory solution.'

'If I understand you correctly, your suggesting that Alfredo should devise something that he himself can't undo.'

'I agree that sounds a bit absurd but it may not require a genius to come to terms with the problem.'

'What exactly do you have in mind then?'

'As an Inspector I am not encouraged to offer solutions in case my recommendations subsequently fail and my Department thus becomes liable for my actions in law.'

'I see, you can tell us what's wrong but you can't tell us how to put it right. That is a bureaucratic nicety one really must admire.'

I was really starting to get fed up with this, although of course he had a point, so I replied, 'There are probably a number of options and I am sure that Mario and Alfredo will be examining these. A fairly simple solution is to fix a metal cover over the cross bar that operates the safety valve in such a way that it is free to move up under pressure but cannot be fastened down to prevent the valve opening under pressure as it is designed to do. The cover itself could be held in place by a good padlock. The key to the padlock could be held in your personal possession and only released when the boiler is shut down for essential maintenance purposes.'

'So the Inspector suddenly becomes an engineer is that my understanding?'

'If you look at the makers name plate on the boiler,and the steam engine, you will see that they were manufactured in England by a firm called Mather and Platt of Lancashire. At the age of 16, I was one of the mechanical engineering apprentices employed by that firm, clearly this does not make me an expert but I am familiar with the design features of this kind of machinery.'

The Commandatori then spoke in Italian to Alfredo and Mario and a general discussion took place in which the two girls seemed to take a prominent part. The Commandatori then seemed to sum up whatever consensus had been agreed upon and replied:-

'It seems to us that there are two points to be resolved, first should we accept your recommendation about the safety valve and, secondly, if we accept that recommendation and implement it, what happens about your threatened prosecution?'

Sir, I thought that I had made it clear that I am not in a position to make a specific recommendation.

I have no authority to do that. I have simply made a suggestion as to how you may ensure that hence forth there will be no repetition of the serious offence which came to light in the course of my inspection. My suggestion is entirely in your interest since you will be liable in law if the offence is repeated especially if an explosion occurs resulting in injuries or fatalities. It may well be that when your sons have had time to give the matter careful thought they will come up with a more effective solution, after all Italians are renowned for the elegance of their engineering design. All I am saying is that it would be wise to do something effective and do it immediately. Regarding a prosecution the boiler as it now stands is safe and will remain so provided that the valve mechanism is not interfered with. If I have your firm assurance that the offence will not be repeated and that practical steps will be taken to ensure that the safety valve can not be rendered inoperative, I propose to include in my Inspection Report a formal warning which will not lead to a prosecution.

In a more relaxed even friendly way the Commandatori replied that I could have his firm assurance on these matters and suggested that we should all have some coffee. In the course of a more general conversation the Commandatorri asked what was my impression of the mine and farm not as a Labour Officer but perhaps as an engineer. I replied that I was really impressed with most of what I had seen and that it must be gratifying for him personally to see such a satisfactory outcome to what must have been many years of sustained hard work. He smiled and was obviously pleased with this response which he had doubtless heard many times before. This seemed a good moment to leave so after thanking the Commandatorri's wife for her kind hospitality and saying goodbye to the rest of the family and collecting my gear and gun we were ready to move on. I had noticed that on the map a secondary road was marked which if viable would could across country in a south easterly direction to join the North South Road and probably save something like 60 miles off the journey to Kondoa Irangi. I asked Mario's advice about the state of this road and in particular if could recommend it bearing in mind that the truck did not have four wheel drive. He seemed to think we should manage alright but pointed out that the road crossed a very wide 'mbuga' (marshy swamp) which made it impassable in the rains. Although the rains were expected there had been no evidence of the heavy thunder storms which usually preceded the rains so, as I was planning on being in Kondoa that evening, I thought it was worth the risk.

BOGGED DOWN IN THE MBUGA

After checking the truck and being satisfied that we had enough petrol to get us to Kondoa, where we could fill up before leaving for Dodoma, we found the track without any difficulty. For the first thirty miles or so we made good progress although the road was deep sand in places and we had to reduce speed quite a bit. According to the map we would have to cross part of the Rift valley where the land dropped to below 3,000 feet and this doubtless would be where we would run in to the Mbulu Mbuga which would be hot and humid. It was evident that this was a little used track through sparsely occupied land, due no doubt to the presence of tetse fly, but doubtless interesting game country. Most of the time we were travelling through thorn scrub and odd patches of open savannah. In the mid-afternoon this was not a good time to be spotting game but Maloda would be keeping a good lookout nevertheless. As we descended into the valley we could see the mbuga in the far distance, a flat stretch of light green reeds reaching out as far as the eye could see. There was no problem keeping to the track and there was some evidence that a heavy vehicle had been travelling ahead of us. Eventually the red murram soil turned to black cotton soil usually associated with marshland and the as the track entered the reeds I was surprised to find that they were about six to eight feet tall. There was only one narrow track across the mbuga and the view was restricted to the track that lay ahead but in the far distance there was some evidence of wild fowl well out of shooting distance but from time to time a flight of duck would pass quickly overhead. There was no wind and the heat became fairly oppressive as we moved farther into the mbuga so too were the flies, mostly mosquitoes much larger than usual but hopefully not malaria carrying. The ground was slightly marshy but not sufficient to cause any real problems.

We travelled about six miles into the mbuga with little evidence
that we were reaching the end. In places we had come across signs
that trucks had sunk into the damp soil and there were deep pits
where people had obviously been obliged to dig their vehicles out.
Where this had happened other vehicles had attempted a
diversion off the track into the reeds in order to avoid getting
bogged down in the same place. We were obliged to adopt the
same tactics on two occasions and although the going was pretty
soft we were glad to get back on to the track which was marginally
drier. The third time this happened we really got into trouble as
we were only doing about five miles an hour in bottom gear and
the rear wheels started to spin and dig in to the soft wet soil until
we lost traction completely. We had a drill for this sort of
situation although the problem was usually deep soft sand. There
were two six foot planks in the back of the truck and using the
Tanganyika Jack we could jack up the back wheels put the planks
under the wheels and with wheels resting on the planks we could
usually get out. But this was very different, all the ground was
soft and muddy and when the jack was operated it just sank down
into the mud instead of lifting the vehicle. The only option we had
was to put the spare wheel under the base of the jack to provide
a bigger bearing surface and this seemed to work pretty well.
However, when Abdullah attempted to drive forward the wheels
still spun even when resting on the planks. By jacking up the rear
wheels we had put more weight on the front and the front wheels
had now sunk quite deeply into the mud; we needed two more
planks which we didn't have.

In situations like this it seemed that the team quickly ran short of
ideas. Abdullah saw his role as strictly that of a driver, he would
drive the truck as long as it would go but if it stopped for some
reason the problem then became someone else's. Aron was very
good at getting things done but he needed clear directions as to
what was required and was certainly not mechanically minded.
The Messengers were interested spectators until told what to do
although Maloda was much more self-reliant and would get
involved with possible solutions. But on this occasion he confined
himself to remarking that he thought the mbuga was slowly filling
up with water which was certainly a worrying thought. One thing

was quite clear and that was that there was very little hope of getting help from elsewhere as the chances of another vehicle reaching us was so remote as to be beyond consideration. The one thing we did have in abundance was good tall strong reeds and each of the messengers had pangas so I set them to work cutting thick bunches of reeds about nine inches thick and bound tightly with reeds Maloda taking charge of this operation. In the meantime we set about removing the spare wheel and jack from the back to the front of the vehicle and jacking up the front wheels clear of the mud. As soon as the Messengers completed a bunch of reeds these were placed in front of the back and front wheels to make a track which, hopefully, would get us back on to the main track.

It took about an hour before we had enough bundles of reeds to make a satisfactory path for the wheels to grip on and by this time we were all sweating, covered in mud and seriously fly bitten. I had also been keeping an eye on the water level which seemed to be only about an inch below the surface of the mud. Just as we were about to put the whole project to the test, with everybody standing behind the truck ready to push, Maloda came up with another helpful remark – 'you usually get plenty of buffalo in reed beds like this'. I decided to do the driving since it was going to be a matter of gently feeling a way forward letting the clutch out very carefully and not accelerating too soon. As soon as I sounded the horn they had been told to push and with the truck in bottom gear it gradually started to move forward slowly building up speed. It worked out better than I thought it might and we were only about twelve yards short of the main track when the back wheels started to spin again. At least now we had a tried and tested procedure for extracting the truck and it was now a matter of repeating the process but we would need more reed bundles although we could still use the undamaged ones. While this was going on I walked along the main track for about two hundred yards to see if the ground was likely to improve. There was still no sign that we were approaching the end of the mbuga, even when I was standing on the top of the cab. However, judging from the state of the track it did appear to be slightly less muddy and the ground seemed to be rising slightly which was encouraging. On the second attempt we did much better and I was able to get the truck back on the main track and keep it moving forward at about five miles an hour for about 400 yards the team trudging slowly behind. The Jack and spare wheel had been loaded into the back of the truck before the second attempt and two of the Messengers had now brought up the planks so we were ready to go. After about another 300yards we came across an old five-ton truck buried about three feet down in the mud apparently a victim of the last rains. Most of the moveable parts had been taken away and it was clear that the truck had found its own graveyard. As we started to move off there was a distant rumbling of thunder in the direction of the Mbulu mountains with ever darkening skies and occasional flashes of lightning. It was obvious that a tropical storm was in progress to the north of us and that the expected rains had now started. In due course massive amounts of surface water would flash over the plain into the mbuga from which we seemed to have just managed to extricate ourselves in time. The prospect of having to notify Headquarters in Dar es Salaam that I had managed to lose the truck didn't stand thinking about.

RETURN VIA KONDOA IRANGI

Clearing the mbuga and climbing up out of the Rift valley we were back into bush country again with just about an hour before darkness set in. We had a spare Jerrycan of water so I told Abdullah to stop to give us a chance to clean up since our feet legs and arms were covered in thick black smelly mud. Our shoes when sluiced off would quickly dry as would Aron's and my stockings but Abdullah, who always wore slacks, was in a real mess but would probably be able to sort something out when we reached Kondoa. Having resumed our journey still on the bush track we came across plenty of game in the distance, giraffe, antelope, zebra and warthog. Eventually there was a thumping on the cab which indicated that Maloda had spotted something which was probably worth a shot so we slowed to a halt and I loaded the gun. Maloda said there were three Thompson's gazelle which we had passed but not noticed about two hundred yards down the track in fairly open country which meant a quiet stalk back down the road and then off into the bush. Maloda, about ten yards in front of me, suddenly crouched down and waved me to follow slowly and quietly. Having reached him I couldn't see a thing despite the fact that he was pointing to a clump of thorn scrub about 80 yards away. After staring for some time I suddenly saw an ear flick and a slight movement as three female antelope moved out of the bush into more open space. They seemed to be unaware of our presence and as there seemed to be no wind to speak of there was every chance of a good shot. Maloda very slowly and quietly moved in such a way that I could rest the gun on his back as I took aim on the smaller of the three.

My first shot was a direct hit, we both heard the thump has the bullet found its mark and the antelope leapt about two feet up in the air before falling on it's side its legs thrashing as it tried to regain its feet. It was lying in short grass but I was able to get off a second shot which also registered a hit. After my second shot

Maloda jumped forward shouting 'Piga, Piga' and raced off towards the kill and by the time I reached him he was holding it by its back legs which were kicking feebly. It was obvious that it was dying from a lung shot, my second shot had struck it the top of its back leg probably breaking the bone. The other messengers had now arrived and Maloda was holding it up saying 'Amekufa bado' – It will soon be dead. He then asked he should 'Jinja' and I said yes quickly so he cut its throat thus shortening the pain and making it possible for Abdullah to eat the meat without contravening his Muslim obligations.

The team were all delighted at the prospect of meat for supper and the effect on them all was really remarkable. Before the antelope was shot they were tired, wet, and had had a long and troublesome day and still a long journey ahead of them. Now, with plenty of fresh meat as their main meal tonight they were really animated and cheerful. The drive down the North / South Road, mainly in the dark, was tiring but uneventful. We stopped at a small hoteli to give Aron a break and were able to get tea and bananas which were welcome as we had had nothing to eat since breakfast. As we resumed our journey the weather became hot and oppressive with that strange atmosphere which precedes the onset of the African rains and which changes dramatically when the first rain falls. As we drove in the dark the only signs of life was an occasional pair of eyes reflected in the headlight beam of some animal, probably hyena, and from time to time night-jars flying up from the road at the very last second just avoiding being smashed by the truck.

The Government Rest House at Kondoa Irangi was located on a slight rise about a quarter of a mile before reaching the town. It was built in the form of two well constructed Rondavals linked together by a fly netted veranda which served as a lounge / dining room. It was sparsely furnished with two single beds in each Rondaval, chairs and table on the veranda and a European style toilet, sink and shower at the rear. The Cook / Houseboy, who looked after the rest house, lived in his own room attached to the cookhouse about ten yards behind the Rest House. Fortunately no other guests were present and he confirmed that none were

expected. The Houseboy, named Juma, quickly lit the fire under
the outside hot water boiler where there was also a standpipe with
running clean water so we could all get a decent wash and remove
what was left of the mud from the mbuga. I had noticed on
previous safaris that the team took every opportunity to get a
good wash at the end of each day and Abdullah would also
manage to perform whatever ablutions were appropriate to his
special needs. The team had the option of going into Kondoa to
find accommodation or to stay at the Rest House . Aron opted to
stay in the other Rondaval and Abdullah,by choice would sleep in
the cab of the truck. The Messengers said that they preferred to
sleep on the front veranda and they were all anxious to skin and
dress out the antelope and to get it roasted over an open fire so
two of them disappeared into the bush to collect firewood. In the
meantime Maloda set about butchering the carcass but without
too much finesse. The general rule at Government Rest Houses
was that visitors brought their own food and the Cook / Houseboy
would be available to cook it. In my case I had nothing to cook
but we did have tea, coffee and canned milk so he was able to
produce a welcome hot drink in short order. Juma kept a few
chickens behind the cookhouse and was able to offer fresh eggs so
I accepted his offer of an omelette which turned out surprisingly
well. So far as the team was concerned, the fire was blazing nicely
and they had placed pieces of meat on stakes of wood over the fire
to roast. The only thing that was missing to make them really
happy was beer. Since there was a pombe shop in Kondoa selling
maize beer I asked Abdullah to drive in to get four large cartons
of pombe and a coca-cola for himself since his religion forbade
him alcohol. I told Maloda to save me a back leg as we were only
half a days drive from home and Wyn would welcome a change
from the usual goats meat. He proposed that his second wife
should take care of the cleaning and curing of the skin as she was
very good at this but when I asked him about a previous skin he
answered rather shiftily that these things take a long time. In fact
I never saw either of them and have a feeling that he has a ready
market for such things. After supper I settled down to write my
report on the inspections I had carried out in Singida and at the
Gold Mine and Farm. Judging from the noise coming from the
group round the fire they were certainly enjoying themselves. I

never ceased to be amazed at the amount of meat they could consume and there was every possibility that before morning they would have consumed everything edible on the carcass – the Messengers would eat the liver when it was almost raw. There was also the sound of African drums coming from Kondoa where some kind of 'ngoma' was taking place, probably celebrating the onset of the rains, and the cries of the women 'ululating' and whistles blowing provided an appropriate backdrop to the laughter coming from the group round the fire. As I was settling down to sleep brilliant flashes of lightening lit up the sky and loud almost deafening burst of thunder reverberated across the land indicating that somewhere not too far away the rains had already started. I was awakened at about 2.00am by the sound of rain battering on the roof of the Rondaval and falling in a cascade on to the compound in front. The Messengers, who had chosen to sleep on the veranda, had dived into the back of the truck and lowered the canvas side curtains to keep out the rains. As I lay awake listening to the downpour I wondered what effect this must be having on the North / South Road and our prospects for travelling tomorrow. I was also conscious of our fortunate escape from the 'mbuga' which would be flooding at an alarming rate under this deluge and had we not managed to get out there would have been no hope whatsoever of recovering the truck. Early the next morning the thunder had abated but the rain continued to fall without let up. The air was unbelievably fresh and stimulating as though Africa had suddenly thrown off its hot, dusty, oppressive atmosphere and been suddenly born again with a sharp, spring-like new lease of life. Everybody felt refreshed, even though we were soaking wet, the water was warm and the team were full of smiles. In what yesterday was semi-desert country the earth seemed to breathe and new green shoots appeared as if by magic. Growing at a phenomenal rate flowers of every description soon appeared and so too did frogs and insects such as flying ants in their thousands. Emaciated cattle stood silent and unmoving in the deluge, water pouring over them ridding them of ticks and other parasites as they anticipated the prospect of good grazing. For other creatures the rains were by no means welcome, rain water entered the monsoon ditches at the sides of the roads flushing out the culverts and drainage pipes.

Snakes, scorpions, and rodents were washed out from their normally dry sandy hideouts into the open and became targets for predatory birds taking advantage of their sudden exposure. For the Wagogo the rains were long awaited and especially welcome as 'Shambas' had been ploughed and seeds sown in anticipation. For them the more rain the better although the traditional Gogo house was built with a flat earth roof about a foot thick and too much rain would be soaked in to the point where the roof would sometimes collapse with disastrous results for the occupants. It was evident that the rain had set in for some time and that travelling by road would become more difficult. However, the North / South Road was probably the best maintained in the Territory and it would take us direct to Dodoma without any diversions, so, with reduced speed and special care we should have no difficulty. We would have to start as early as possible but first I had to complete the usual courtesy of signing the Book at the District Headquarters alerting the District Officer to my presence in his area. On reaching the 'Boma' there was a great deal of activity with crowds of Africans milling about and the District Officer busy in the middle trying to sort out some kind of crisis. It turned out that during the night the heavy rains had filled up the dry riverbed which passed the end of the town and on the banks of which was built the local prison. The water surging past the walls had washed away the whole side of the prison building and at 3.00 am the District Officer was awakened by a mob of prisoners complaining that they had nowhere to sleep. No one had even thought of escaping, which seemed to give the lie to the idea that confinement in the 'Hoteli Kingi Georgi', as prisons were generally called, was a prospect best avoided. Apparently two meals a day, guaranteed, and a secure place to sleep with acceptable company, was not something to be rejected out of hand. This was especially the case where inmates took advantage of the prison training programmes which produced brick layers, carpenters, plumbers, and sewing machinists, all of whom were much sought after by employers. In registering for employment at the Labour Office such 'fundis' would insist that it be recorded that they were prison graduates thus establishing their fully trained status. On the journey home we made quite reasonable progress over the first thirty miles or so even though the rain continued without let up. Driving called for special skills and much vigilance as the road was a muddy quagmire particularly dangerous in navigating bends where skids were almost unavoidable and the monsoon ditches at the sides of the road were easy to slide into but hellish to get out of. Travelling too fast was obviously dangerous but so also was going too slow because this gave the rear wheels a chance to sink in to the soft mud and lose traction through wheel spin; about 20 to 25 miles an hour seemed to be the optimum speed. Abdullah and I drove at hourly intervals because of the need for concentration. After about 40 miles we were driving over more open country and the rains seemed to be easing slightly. I stopped to give Aron a break as he was feeling sick but this time perhaps aggravated by the consumption of meat last night. In the far distance we could see a truck of some sort pulled up at the side of the road and we were speculating as to whether it had broken down or was simply stuck in the mud. When we finally reached the truck we discovered that it was stopped because the road in front was completely flooded due to a fast flowing river sweeping across the road. In the dry season this was a sandy riverbed over which the road turned into a concrete strip about 15 feet wide connecting both banks. At intervals of about ten yards there were wooden post about six feet high painted black and white indicating the edge of the strip and the depth of water when, as now, the river filled up and overflowed the road. The vehicle waiting on the bank was a five-ton truck loaded with charcoal and mixed goods driven by a very young Asian lad named Ali. He was accompanied by an African 'turni-boy' named Saidi an assistant who usually sat on the back of the truck to stop people stealing goods and helped to guide the truck when it was reversing or turning round. They were trying to get to Dodoma but had been waiting all night hoping that the water level would subside. When we reached it the water was over a hundred yards wide and flowing very fast and I judged to be about three feet deep according to the marker posts so there was no hope of attempting a crossing until the water level dropped. To make matters worse a large Baobab tree had been uprooted by the current and swept down stream so that it was firmly lodged over the concrete strip blocking the road and when the water level fell this would have to be removed before a crossing could be attempted. On the other bank was a LandRover whose occupants like us were stuck waiting to make a crossing. My hopes of reaching Dodoma by mid-day were now totally diminished and it was a matter for speculation as to how long it might be before we could attempt to move the tree prior to making a crossing. For the moment there was little we could do except wait as there was no possibility of finding a diversion elsewhere but in the last half hour there was some sign that the rain was easing off a little. Maloda sharpened a stick and pushed it into the edge of the water so that we could measure what ever fall in the water level there might be. At Aron's suggestion we managed to get a fire going by scrounging charcoal off Ali and we set about brewing tea. With the fire going nicely Maloda and the other Messengers were having a fairly animated discussion in Chigogo out of which came the suggestion that we might as well cook the remaining leg of the antelope has it would not in this heat survive the delayed journey home. I found this difficult to resist and it wasn't too long before the meat was roasting nicely to every ones satisfaction.

As soon as the water level started to fall we would have to devise some method of removing the tree from the middle of the causeway but we had plenty of time to work something out. It would be far too heavy to push over the causeway, even with the current to help us, as the roots were sticking up above the water and these would certainly be lodged against the concrete strip below the water. The only option seemed to be to wade out to the tree and chop the trunk clean through and then push each half off the edge of the causeway. We had a good axe and it turned out so too did Ali, the limiting factor would be the water level and the speed of the current but, on the plus side Baobabs are soft pulpy wood as opposed to hard wood and with sharp axes it would not be too difficult to cut through. It would take time and it would be hard work standing up in the current but I couldn't see any other way of proceeding. We had a good tow- rope and Ali had a good length of chain but joined together there was no way that they would reach out to the tree. The two Europeans with the Landrover on the far bank had now erected a tent and produced two camp chairs and appeared content to await events as they sat drinking beer.

As we were waiting the team were discussing the events of last night and the amount of meat they had managed to consume. Between them they seemed to have eaten everything that was edible and in my judgement some things which were decidedly not. According to Maloda one of his wives was a real 'fundi' at cleaning and curing skins and he offered to have this one done for me. He claimed that she had done many skins for one of my predecessors, Bwana Robson-Gibson who, I was never allowed to forget, was a crack shot, never missed anything and shot every thing in sight. I had taken up this offer on a previous occasion but as yet no end product had emerged. I reminded him of this but he rather shiftily replied that these things take time if they are done properly and I would get the skin 'Bado' – a swahili word meaning later, but often meaning never.

While we were sat together talking I asked Aron if he had ever heard about the Kings African Rifles fighting a major battle in this part of Kondoa during the 1914-18 war in E. Africa. He replied that he had never heard of it but that one of his uncles had fought with the British against the Germans in that war. He then asked what was remarkable about the Kondoa battle and I started to explain that the big guns used by the British and the Germans had fought a previous battle in the Indian Ocean. Aron, whose interest was now roused asked if I would tell them what happened. Maloda, who had been listening to this but failed to understand what was being said, asked Aron if he would translate what I was saying into Swahili so they could all understand. I then found myself relating what must have seemed to them as a highly unlikely story of how a British war ship named the Pegasus was undergoing repairs in Zanzibar harbour. A German battle cruiser named the Konigsberg then steamed into the Zanzibar Channel and fired its ten 4.1 inch guns into the Pegasus. The Pegasus was able to reply with its eight 4 inch guns firing back at the Konigsburg but the Pegasus was seriously damaged, a lot of sailors were killed and it eventually sank. Soon afterwards the Konigsberg ran short of coal to fuel its steam engines and had to hide in the mouth of the Rufji river in southern Tanganyika. The British were able to recover three guns from the Pegasus and fit them on to wheeled carriages specially made at the railway workshop in Mombasa and they were then taken to Kilimanjaro where they formed the 10th Heavy Battery under the command of General Deventer. He led the British army from Kilimanjaro down the North / South road (the road we were now on) to fight the Germans at Kondoa.

The German battle cruiser Konigsberg was eventually shelled by two British warships in the Rufiji River and totally destroyed. However, the guns were recovered and mounted on carriages and one of them was brought by the German army to take part in the battle at Kondoa. So, in the middle of Africa, hundreds of miles from the sea, the guns of the Pegasus and the Konigsberg fired at each other again and one of the shells from the Pegasus nearly killed the German General, Von Lettow Vorbeck. The team listened to this saga very closely and were really interested to hear about the Wadarchi (Germans) but as the messengers had never seen the sea and had no concept as to what a warship looked like I had to sketch these for them in my note book together with drawings of a field gun. I also explained that dragging the guns across the land from the Rufiji to Dar es Salaam was very hard work and they used many Africans as forced labour who were made to do this whether they wanted to or not. When I had finished Elio, who was probably the quietest among them, suddenly became quite animated and had a great deal to say but in Chigogo. When this was translated it turned out that his father saw the Wadarchi when they came through Ugogo during the war and, though most people ran away in fear, his father and some others hid, and watched the Germans dig a hole and bury something. After the Germans had left and before the British arrived they dug up whatever it was and then dug another hole and hid it again. After the war they dug it up again and took it to the Bwana District Commissioner and it was now in the Boma in Dodoma. In the light of these surprising relevations I made a point of enquiring about this and found that the 'Thing' was a breach block from a 4.1inch German field gun which the Germans had quickly disabled during a hasty retreat.

This surprising contribution from Elio underlines one of the key aspects of tribal culture. Since nothing is written down, everything is endlessly discussed and remembered in great detail. The African night is long and sometimes menacing, it is dark at 6.30 p.m. when small stock and cattle have to be secured against predators, fires lit and compounds made safe. There are no books and no light to read by and very limited access to radio because of the difficulty of affording and obtaining batteries. Everything that has happened is discussed in detail and very little forgotten, or for that matter forgiven. It was not unusual for an African to expect to carry on a conversation which may have terminated weeks ago but which one may have completely forgotten about. This was the first time Elio had ever addressed me directly but he used to watch me carefully almost as though afraid that I might suddenly do him some harm. He would usually manage to keep someone else between us and would gaze at me as though I was something in a zoo that might at any time do something ridiculous or perhaps amusing. His general approach was rather like the reactions of small children when, if we stopped the truck in a small remote village, they would run up to satisfy their curiosity and, as I stepped out of the truck, suddenly be confronted with their worst nightmare. When I was a small child and behaving badly my mother, but more often my elder sisters, would claim that the 'bogey-man' would get me; for me the 'bogy-man' though never described was something alarming and probably black. African mothers dealing with the same problem would say to small children the 'Mzungu' – European – will get you. So, as I stepped out of the truck there I was, white skin, long straight hair the colour of grass, and worst of all blue eyes – no wonder they ran back to their mothers, fearful and sometimes on the verge of tears. It was fairly clear that whilst Elio found my behaviour interesting and worth watching the bogy-man was ever present and there were no grounds for dropping ones guard.

After about two hours the flow of the river seemed to be slackening and according to Maloda's stick the water level was falling. Carrying the axe as a walking stick I waded slowly along the concrete causeway keeping close to the black and white marker posts. The current was still fairly strong but not sufficient to sweep me off my feet and I was able to reach the tree without any problem. It was lodged diagonally across the causeway and had been prevented from floating over the causeway by its roots which were lodged under water by the side of the concrete strip. The tree trunk was just over two feet thick about half of it above the water level. If it was chopped in two each part of the trunk could probably be pushed over the edge of the causeway even though one part would have to be pushed against the current. I waded back and discussed the situation with Aron and Ali both of whom thought it worth a try but Ali claiming to be a non-swimmer said he couldn't help but volunteered the services of his turnie-boy.

With two axes only two people could work together at a time so Abdullah and I took the first shift wading out together. Since Abdullah could not swim and was understandably pretty nervous I tied the tow-rope round his waist and held onto it until I could fasten it firmly to the marker post nearest to the tree. Standing either side of the trunk we started to chop into it and found ourselves making good progress as the wood was soft and after about fifteen minutes we had managed to cut through about a quarter of the trunk. We waded back and it was then the turn of Aron and Maloda neither of whom could swim and were extremely nervous. I fastened the tow-rope round both of them and we all three waded out together and I again fastened the rope to the marker post. I stayed with them which seemed to give them confidence and it wasn't long before they were making really good progress cutting well past the half way mark. As we all waded back to the bank I was thinking that it was now the turn of Elio and Rumigo who were both pretty light weight and were obviously frightened of the water and non swimmers. I decided that it would be too risky to let them make an attempt so I went out again but this time with Saidi the turnie-boy. He was a strong, heavily built member of the Sukumu tribe, brought up on a fish diet in the Lake Province, who volunteered his services without hesitation. As we waded out I could see that the two Europeans on the opposite bank had set up a tripod and camera and were busy filming the whole performance. I waved to them to come and help but the only response was a shrug of the shoulders.

Between us we made good progress and after fifteen minutes sustained chopping the tree trunk broke in to two halves one part swinging round in the current and drifting clear of the cause way. Saidi and I waded back to the bank for a break and to contemplate the next move which might prove to be the most difficult.

Checking the stick it was evident that the water level had fallen by about six inches but the current was still fairly strong and we would have to push the trunk up against it. As a first step I waded out with Abdullah Aron and Saidi and having made them secure with the tow rope we all tried to push the trunk over the edge of the causeway but could scarcely move it.

We needed more manpower so I waved to the two men on the other bank who were still filming to come out and give us a hand. Nothing came of this so there was no alternative but to call on Rumigo and Elio. Reluctantly they agreed so I waded out with them slowly, one on each arm, while the others shouted encouragement. I fastened the tow rope round their waist, since Abdullah and Aron seemed confident enough without it, and together with a concerted effort, Maloda shouting a tribal call, we managed to move the trunk about three feet. Taking our time from Maloda we continued to make progress but on the last push the trunk swung round slightly and Elio whose hand was under water cried out that his hand was trapped. We immediately tried to lift the trunk so he could pull it out but failed to move it. This was serious, I couldn't see how badly his hand was trapped because it was under water but I told him to stop pulling as he may be doing more harm than good. I waded towards the people on the other bank and shouted for their help but they refused. Things were now getting a bit desperate but Elio remained calm and seemed to think we would soon have him free. I suddenly remembered the two planks in the truck and asked Saidi to fetch them. With these set in place under the trunk and a concerted heave on them Elio was able to pull his hand free to every ones relief and the trunk slid back off the causeway. Elio right hand was wet and bleeding freely and it was apparent that he had lost most of his little finger but there was no other damage. Back at the truck I was able to wash the wound with clean water and, having treated it with iodine, applied a good tight dressing aimed at stopping the bleeding. I also put a sling round his neck so that his arm could be supported in a comfortable position. Although it was obviously painful he seemed quite stoical about losing part of his finger and cheered up considerably as Aron explained that he would be given money under the Workmens Compensation Act. As soon as the water fell to a reasonable depth the way was now clear to attempt a crossing.

CROSSING THE FLOODED IRANGI

We waited for about another hour in which time we made a brew and recovered the two planks and the tow-rope. By then the water level had dropped to about 18 inches but there was still a fairly fast current. A more worrying development was the heavy black rain clouds which were building up to the north east and the lightening and rumbles of thunder which suggested that heavy rain was falling not too far away and this would doubtless feed into the river. The worry was how long it would take to reach us and could we get across before this happened. Fortunately the truck had a fairly high wheel-base and the engine could still perform in about 18 inches of water. However, as a precaution I tied my toilet bag, which was waterproof over the distributor and wound insulating tape round the terminals of the sparkplugs and battery terminals to prevent them getting wet. As we started the crossing I asked Abdullah if he would like me to drive, unusually he seemed slightly indignant at this suggestion and said he would be alright. This was strange as in awkward situations he was only too happy for me to drive and be responsible if anything went wrong. I told him to drive at about ten miles an hour at a constant speed and to keep in first gear. I also warned him to keep within about 2 feet of the marker posts during the crossing to make sure he did not drive off the causeway.

As we entered the water everything seemed fine and the weight of the truck seemed to hold against the pressure of the current. By the time we were about a third of the way across water entered the cab under the bottom of the doors but this was not a problem. Then water came up round the clutch and brake pedals wetting Abdullah's feet and his immediate reaction was to take his foot of the accelerator and with the truck in gear the engine stalled. Worse still, with the truck stationary the water, pressure slowly forced the front end across the causeway so that the offside wheel went over the edge. Abdullah seemed to go into some sort of a trance, frozen behind the wheel, and I had a problem getting him to move so that I could drive. Fortunately the engine started first time but when I put it in reverse gear and tried to back up to get the wheel on to the causeway the back wheels spun and the truck would not move. We all waded back to the bank feeling pretty frustrated, particularly myself as I realised that I should have insisted on driving myself notwithstanding Abdullah's assurances. The only hope now was to get a tow-rope on the back axle and using Ali's lorry pull the truck back until the front wheel was back on the causeway. Ali agreed to this provided that I would drive so I drove his vehicle within towing distance of the truck fastened the tow-rope between the two. I told Abdulah to start up and put the truck in reverse when I sounded the horn on Ali's lorry. All that happened was that the truck was pulled backwards about ten feet and then the tow rope broke. It was obvious that Abdullah, who was still 'switched off' had not attempted to get the front wheel back on the causeway by holding the steering wheel firmly in the right hand down position. Fortunately, Saidi could drive, although he didn't have a licence, and once we had connected Ali's chain in place as a tow-rope we went through the same procedure again, this time with success. Having disconnected the chain and given it to Saidi we were now ready to make a second attempt but before starting I agreed with Ali that if we got across I would wade back and drive his truck over too. The second crossing went as planned, although I was surprised at the pressure of the water in mid stream, we were all soaking wet by this stage and spent some time sorting ourselves out. After wading back I was able to drive Ali's truck over without any difficulty, it was heavy enough to withstand the water pressure and its double back wheels ensured plenty of traction. During this performance the two Europeans on the far bank, who turned out to be German tourists, had been filming the whole process almost as though the whole episode had been laid on for their benefit. They dismantled their tent and camera and were now preparing to make the crossing, they offered no apologies for failing to help or thanks for clearing the tree trunk. When I asked why they chose not to help they claimed not to understand English so that was that. By this time I was soaking wet as I had gone over the side of the causeway to examine the truck's front wheel and the water there was about five feet deep. My wet clothes from crossing the mbuga were in the back of the truck to which I now added the ones I was now wearing the only remaining option now was to wear my pyjamas; a spectacle that evoked huge grins from the team. As we removed the water proofing from the engine and I recovered my toilet bag the Germans were now preparing to make their crossing. With a modern LandRover, a four wheel drive vehicle, they shouldn't have much of a problem so now it was our turn to watch them. In the meantime the water level seemed to have risen slightly and the current in mid stream would be marginally faster. They entered the water slightly faster than I would have advised and seem to speed up as they were about halfway across with consequence that both the near side wheels came off the causeway on the down stream side and the Landrover came to a halt. The reaction from the team was smiles all round as we watched the offside door of the cab open and the two Germans emerged clinging to the top of the cab. They promptly started waving to us and the team responded by waving back, given the masterly display of inactivity they had exhibited in response to my calls for help there was no suggestion from anyone that we should go out to help them. Ali and Saidi seemed to take the same view but when I suggested to Ali that he could probably charge them £50 to tow them out he had second thoughts but only for a moment. We were now ready to start the last leg home but I thought I should put it to the vote as to whether we should stay to help. They were all totally against, arguing that when we were in trouble they refused to help us, so why should we help them. I suspect that in that mood even if I had ordered them to help I would only have got only token support. Just as we were ready to move, a large East African Railways truck arrived on the far bank so at least the Germans would not be left alone.

When I checked Elio's hand it seemed to have stopped bleeding so we set off for Dodoma and arrived home in the dark but without incident. Elio was taken to the hospital where stitches were put into what was left of his finger and with a new dressing and a tetanus injection he seemed to be fine. As a corollary to this safari, when I reached home Joseph collected all my wet clothes from the back of the truck and washed them the next day. He brought the basin in which he had been washing my wet khaki stockings to show Wyn all the sand and sediment that had been washed out of them. In the sand and gravel there were distinct specks of gold which must have been trapped as I splashed about in the river.

I mentioned this subsequently to a friend who was employed in the Geological Surveys Department and was informed that the presence of gold in that part of Kondoa was not really surprising. The problem so far as exploitation was concerned would be deciding where the main reef from which the gold came was located. This would require a detailed and expensive survey which would require considerable time.

Part 6

PROSECUTIONS IN DODOMA

Reviewing Inspection Reports on local factories left me with the distinct impression that, whilst there was no shortage of reports or threats of 'Last Chance', Final Warning', 'Threats to Close Down', etc. things remained little changed. Most workshops, rice and oil-mills, carpenters and builders, saw-mills, I had inspected revealed that very little had been done by way of safe guarding of machinery or improved working practices design to ensure compliance with the law. It was also evident that the rules restricting the employment of child labour were being ignored. Maloda had picked up a bazaar rumour that a boy aged 11 working in a local factory had lost his leg below the knee and had been taken out to a Mission hospital and the parents paid Shgs 500 by the employer to keep the matter quiet. My own reports following inspections recorded contraventions of the Factories Act, or dangerous working practices, and threatened legal action if remedial action was not taken forthwith. It was fairly obvious that employers regarded me as yet another Labour Officer going through the motions, but in my case with limited experience, who in the course of time will be transferred elsewhere. Action by employers, particularly if it involved expenditure, seldom followed promises to put matters right and dangerous machinery and working practices continued to be the norm. When I discussed this situation with Panjawani and Aron they both seemed to think that things had been like this for years and were not likely to change in the short term. There was nothing in earlier Quarterly Reports to Headquarters to indicate that prosecutions had been undertaken and Panjawani was not aware of any court actions which had taken place during his service in Dodoma. Aron, whose experience in Central Province was almost as limited as my own, said that he had never been called upon to give evidence in a prosecution under the Factories Act in other Provinces. Both of them seemed to confirm the view that Departmental policy although not stated seemed to be based on 'enlightened persuasion' rather than legal sanctions. In response to my earlier enquires Aron had said that in his experience in other Provinces conditions in Dodoma were pretty similar to conditions he had inspected elsewhere. So far as 'Enlightened Persuasion' was concerned I could see little prospect of securing essential improvements through this approach. Factory owners would listen politely to my warnings and observations, offer tea and refreshments and smilingly promises that all will be put in order – no problem. The reality was that nothing happened, my written reports, which Aron or Maloda delivered by hand, were set aside often I suspect unread and things continued unchanged. I could find no case law which might provide guidance in this area and it seemed clear that if I decided to prosecute I might in a sense be setting an unwelcome precedent. However, I put it to both Panjawani and Aron that what was needed to get change was a successful prosecution resulting in a substantial fine, or for continued offence, a prison sentence. I don't think either of them welcomed an initiative on

Wagogo Bride and Bridegroom
(Just Married)

these lines, Aron considering that a failure to get a conviction could do more harm than good. Panjawani agreed with this but he was also concerned that if this kind of action was taken it should be against Muslims and not Hindus'. I think that both of them were influenced to some extent by the fact that I had not yet passed my law exams which of course was a factor I had to keep in mind.

So far as targets were concerned it seemed to me that little would be achieved by prosecuting one or two smaller undertakings where convictions might be easy but sentences would probably turn out to be small fines or warnings. These would set a poor example to the major employing concerns and would be unlikely to secure a real change in attitude. From a review of earlier inspection reports and those I had completed myself two major employing concerns, where contraventions were clear, warnings had been given, but no action taken, were Ranjit Singh, Central Province Woodworking and Building, and Lotus Rice and Oil Mills. The former was the place where it was rumoured that a boy had lost his leg and the latter had been continuously warned about dangerous unfenced machinery.

When I mentioned these to Panjawani he was horrified. These he said were two of the wealthiest men in the township, everybody owed them money, and they had enormous influence on the Town Council. He went on to say that they would certainly seek legal assistance in their defence and might even bring an Advocate up from Dar es Salaam. Aron seemed equally worried and he was aware that I would be calling him as a witness to the hand delivery of my Inspection Reports and to the verbal warnings I had delivered in the course of my inspections. He certainly did not welcome the prospect of being cross examined by the defence Council in Court notwithstanding my assurances that he would only have to confirm proven facts. Against this background I had to think very carefully about the prospects of getting firm convictions. So far as I was aware, neither of the employers had previously been prosecuted for contraventions under the Factories Act before, although Ranjit Singh had appeared in court on a number of occasions in connection with commercial litigation, but both would be regarded as first offenders by the Magistrate. So far as making a case was concerned it seemed to me to be largely a question of fact, that there were dangerous unfenced machines in both cases was self evident and that this situation contravened the relevant Sections of the Factories Act was also a fact easily proven. There were a number of other offences in respect of dangerous, unearthed electrical equipment, inadequate or non-existent fire precautions, unsatisfactory ventilation and the absence of first aid equipment to be taken into account. It would also be a straight forward matter to prove that these offences were long standing and that previous warnings by myself and other Inspectors had been ignored. What was less certain was the availability of suitable evidence over the illegal employment of child labour in the case of the Rice and Oil Mill. Certainly there were under age children working in the Mill when I carried out my inspection but the problem would centre round the ability to prove a child's age. A rough and ready guide in the absence of documentary evidence of date of birth, which in many parts of Africa was non-existent, was to examine the child's teeth – a full set meant that the child was probably over the age of 12 but a good defence advocate would make mincemeat of this kind of evidence. The Employment Ordinance made it an offence to employ children under that age and even above 12 child labour was only permitted under clearly defined conditions i.e. in the company of parents and on tasks usually related to harvesting specific crops. Taking photographs of children in workshops offered some kind of evidence but problems would doubtless arise in trying to get such children into court – there was a very real possibility that they would disappear long before a case was heard. The law, in this case the Employment Ordinance, defined a child as a person under the age of 12 years but this would need to be proved. I had discussed this problem with a friend, who was a local Asian doctor in private practice, and he came up with what to me was a surprising solution. It is generally accepted in medical circles that a pair of bones in the elbow of a child do not join up into a solid joint until about the age of 12 and an X-ray of the arm would demonstrate this. He agreed to appear as an 'Expert Witness' in support of my case provided of course that his fees for such a service would be met by the Court or my

Department. This was certainly tricky since if I was successful, and the Court awarded costs in my favour, there would be no problem but there were no funds available for such a purpose in my Departmental budget; so the costs could be a charge I would have to meet myself. Before deciding what action I should take I sought an interview with the Resident Magistrate regarding the possible timing of such a case and the likely procedure. He quite rightly refused to discuss any of the issues likely to be raised in the case but on the question of Court procedure he advised that I should sit in on prosecutions conducted by the police which would give me a detailed opportunity to see the Court in action. After careful consideration it became obvious to me that if I was to have any impact on the blatant contraventions of the of the Factories Act which typified many employing concerns in the Province simply issuing Inspection Reports was not going to serve. It was also clear that to secure a more responsible attitude on the part of employers a successful, high profile, prosecution could be the catalyst for affecting change. Accordingly I prepared the necessary Complaint Forms and on the basis of these the Court issued the Summonses setting out the Charges and the date of the Court hearing. As Panjawani predicted, an Advocate was engaged to defend the case against the Rice and Oil Mill, but Ranjit Singh elected to defend himself. In the meantime, I sat in Court to gain some experience of court procedures as advised by the Magistrate and was reasonably confident of my ability to lead a prosecution as the case required.

Panjawani was really worried about these proceedings but he was keeping his ear to the ground and picking up local gossip about the case, which, in a small town like Dodoma, was attracting particular attention in the Asian community. The Advocate who would be leading for the defence was reputed to be well equipped with natural cunning and was more than familiar with the off-side rules if he was allowed to get away with them. Aron was also worried over the role he would have to play in giving evidence to support my case and provide evidence of delivering my Inspection Reports to the two accused. He needed some help with this and I carefully went over the questions I would put to him in the Court which would mostly require a simple yes or no in corroboration of what I was leading in evidence. I also had to alert him as to the ways of the Defence Advocate who would try to confuse him. I spent some time on this to build up Aron's confidence and to assure him that he should answer any questions from the Magistrate simply and honestly as there was nothing to fear. Regarding the Advocate, it was impossible to guess what he might ask but where necessary he should not be afraid to say to the Magistrate that he did not understand what the Advocate was asking him to say. As a general rule I advised him to take his time in answering and to try and reply with a simple 'Yes', 'No', or 'I don't know'. We rehearsed these issues fairly thoroughly until Aron felt confident about his role and, although the whole ethos in court proceedings is that witnesses should not be rehearsed, unlike many cases at least he was being rehearsed to tell the truth.

On the day the case was heard the defence Advocate, an Asian of some repute from Dar es Salaam, asked the court for an adjournment on the grounds that his client had not been given sufficient time to prepare his defence. This surprised me and as I was anxious to get the case heard I objected on the grounds that since the date of my inspection and the serving of the summons there had been ample time for an adequate response. I also pointed out that the unsatisfactory conditions in the Rice and Oil Mill were of long standing and, since the defendant had taken no action to remedy them, they remained a constant hazard to the workers involved. To the Advocate's annoyance and my relief the Magistrate upheld my objection and ruled that the case continue. The Court Room was crowded, mostly by Asian traders, many of whom had workshops which were liable to inspection, so they had a direct interest in the final outcome. I was heartened to see that the whole of the Labour Department staff were also in court, Panjawani and Mr. Jonathan as one might expect, but also the driver, Abdullah, Maloda, and all the Messengers including the staff from the Transit Centre. They were all clean and tidy with highly polished Departmental Badges and buttons – I doubt whether they would understand a word of what was going on, since the language of the Court was English, but it was good to have their support nevertheless. This meant that the Department was closed so, much to his disappointment, I had to ask Jonathan to return to the office. Leading the case for the prosecution I referred to the contraventions of the Factories Act I had encountered in the course of a formal inspection I had carried out as part of my duties as a Government appointed Factory Inspector in the premises of the accused. I tabled my Inspection Report in evidence and confirmed that this report had been served on the accused by an Inspector appointed by my Department. I drew the Court's attention to the contraventions listed in detail in the report and my conclusion that these constituted offences under the Factories Act. I also submitted that these were long standing offences, which had been brought to the defendant's notice in previous Inspection Reports undertaken by my predecessors, and I tabled copies of these reports in evidence. I explained to the Court that it was the policy of my Department to secure compliance with the provisions of the Factories Act through advice and persuasion prosecution being a last resort. However, in the case of the defendant he had chosen not to act on such advice and to ignore the contents of the Inspection Reports, in particular those parts of the Report warning him that failure to act would render him liable to prosecution. I asked the Court to accept that, in the interest of the health and safety of the defendant's employees, I have a duty to ensure that the hazards to which they are exposed on a daily basis in the course of their employment are removed.

At this point I noticed Jonathan standing at the back of the Court with a middle-aged European who I didn't recognise but Jonathan was drawing my attention to him and he then withdrew. The Magistrate asked if the Defence wished to make a statement at this stage and in opening the case for the Defence the Advocate submitted that his client had 'No Case to Answer' on two grounds:-

(i) That the offences complained of were in no way unusual and were consistent with common practice in the industry concerned and that no one could reasonably be required to fence a machine if the result was to render the machine inoperative.

And

(ii) That the complaints are based on the views of an inexperienced Inspector, unfamiliar with the conditions of industry in Tanganyika who is only holding a probationary appointment and has yet pass his law examinations.

The Magistrate then said that before he made a decision on the Defence's submission of No Case to Answer he would like to hear if the Prosecution wished to make a response. I was unprepared for this surprising development which called for some quick thinking at short notice. After a slight pause I asked the Court to consider that the two points offered in support of a case of 'No Case to Answer' were inaccurate and misleading. On the first point the Accused was not being asked to fence machinery so as to render it inoperable as claimed, what was required was suitable fencing to protect workers from moving parts such as were in common use in factories in Tanganyika and elsewhere. On the second point the claim about my lack of experience is not relevant since the complaints against the defendant have also been made by my predecessors as set out in the Inspection Reports before the Court.

These Officers have extensive experience over many years in most Provinces in the Territory. In addition the defendant's Council takes no account of the practical experience I have in engineering and workshop management which satisfied the Tanganyika authorities as to my suitability in making my appointment which has been formally 'Gazetted' in accordance with Government Regulations.

The Magistrate then ruled that he was not convinced that there was no case to answer and directed that the case continue accordingly. He then asked the accused how he pleaded and, after a short discussion with his client, the Defendant replied 'Not Guilty'. At the Magistrate's request I then carried on making the detailed case for the Prosecution by going, item by item, through my Inspection Report underlining each offence as appropriate. It was now Aron's turn to give evidence to corroborate what I had been saying so I called him as a witness for the Prosecution.

Earlier in the morning he had been vomiting which was not unusual for Aron when we were travelling in the truck but on this occasion it was probably due to nerves as he awaited the ordeal of appearing in Court. We had given him a drink of hot sweet tea before going in to Court and this seemed to settle him a bit. He was well turned out, uniform clean and pressed, brasses polished and wearing shoes he normally reserved for church on Sundays. In the event he performed exceptionally well, shouting out his evidence in a loud parade ground voice and seemingly confident and in control. For reasons best known to himself the defence Counsel seemed slightly intimidated by Aron's performance and did not seek to cross examine him so Aron was allowed to stand down. In effect this brought me to the end of the prosecutions case for the four counts under the Factories Act

At this point the defence Council started his cross-examination of my evidence. I expected that he would go through my submission item by item challenging most of my evidence and calling witnesses to support the defence's case where appropriate. To my surprise he returned to the question of my lack of experience and my ability to perform the duties of a Factory Inspector. As I entered the witness box he seemed to be in close consultation with the Defendant and some other person, whose identity I was unaware of, but who seemed to have a dominant role in defence proceedings. He opened up the cross-examination by saying 'Mr Glynn, I would like to take you back to your earlier remarks about your appointment. Would you be good enough to tell the Court what precisely this experience amounts to since I am informed that you were a professional soldier before your present appointment.'

I replied that, as explained earlier, my experience and qualifications are sufficient to satisfy the Appointing Authorities as to my suitability for the post I now hold that is a Labour Officer / Factory Inspector. I then went on to say that if the Court really needs this information may I point out that as a professional soldier I held the rank of Captain in the Royal Mechanical and Electrical Engineers and served as the Officer in Charge of a Military Workshop employing a wide range of Craftsmen and Technicians servicing guns, transport, radar equipment, generators and electrical mechanical machinery. The Advocate seemed nonplussed at this reply but went on to ask if I had any other experience in the engineering field. I replied that I had served on the Directing Staff of the Military Collage of Science teaching senior officers on the Advance Technical Staff Course a pass in which is equated to a BSc in Mechanical Engineering. His look of frustration seemed to indicate that this was not what he expected to hear as it was apparent that his defence strategy was to discredit my competence to make judgements on technical matters.

He now decided to abandon the attack on my technical abilities and to focus on my limited local experience.

'Mr. Glynn, would I be right in saying that you have been in the Territory for less than 12 months?'

'That is correct.'

'Would you agree with me that it is highly unusual to find a Government officer with limited or no experience in the Territory exercising powers under Government legislation?'

'Your Honour, I am not sure where this line of questioning is going to lead us but surely the Counsel for the defence must be aware that a wide range of Government Officers, including doctors, veterinary officers, surveyors, architects, even lawyers, are appointed to posts in Government service, none of whom can claim previous service in the Territory, but nevertheless are quite capable of carrying out their statutory duties. I put it to the Court that my case is in no way an exception.'

At this point the Magistrate indicated that there seemed to be little point in carrying this line of questioning any further and adjourned the hearing until 2.30pm.

As we dispersed the European whom Johnathan had brought to Court introduced himself as a visiting Factory Inspector, based at Labour Headquarters in Dar es Salaam, who was now on a tour of Provincial Departments to offer help and advice on factory matters. I had not received any notification of such a visit but the timing of it couldn't have been more convenient. Here was the ideal Expert Witness with years of experience in the Territory whose evidence would be absolutely beyond question. It turned out that he had driven down from Arusha in the Northern

Province the previous day and spent the night in the Railway Hotel, hoping to catch me in the office this morning. The timing of this visit was brilliant, if unexpected, and my prospects for securing a successful outcome to the prosecutions rose immediately. I suggested that we should make a quick inspection of the Rice and Oil Mill and Singh's Workshop, review my reports on both premises, and I could then call him as an 'Expert Witness' during the afternoon court session. However, my optimism was short lived as the Inspector, who was a fairly dour, elderly, former ships engineer, clearly didn't welcome the proposition that he should appear in court.

I should have thought that it was obvious that I needed all the help I could get but he claimed that he would need more time to study my Inspection Reports and would need to carry out a comprehensive inspection of the factory premises. This was disappointing but I pressed on suggesting that I could ask the Court for an adjournment until the next day on the grounds that an important prosecution witness had now become available. He didn't like that either and then put forward the surprising view that there was no point in his participating in the case as he already had extensive experience of court cases but that I was the one who needed this experience particularly in the early part of my career. He could see that I found this difficult to accept and that I was also greatly disappointed but it was obvious that discussion on these lines had reached an impasse. After a pause I then asked him what was the purpose of his visit to which he replied that he was calling on Provincial Offices to discuss problems in the factories inspection area and to give advice where needed. I replied that, as he could see, I had a problem – how to succeed in my prosecutions, however, since he was unwilling to offer practical help what advice would he like to offer. His response was to the effect that he would need to study the whole case in detail before he could reach any sort of conclusions. He went on to say that he had an appointment in Kilosa, his next destination, in the morning and that if he was to avoid driving in the dark he would have to leave fairly shortly. In the event he checked out of the hotel and was gone by 2.00p.m. Panjawani, who had listened to most of this, contacted a friend at the hotel and learned that the Inspector was originally booked in for two nights Kilosa notwithstanding. I subsequently learned that he had never conducted a prosecution under the Factories Act or even appeared as a witness in a court case. As the case resumed in the afternoon it quickly became apparent that the Defence had changed their strategy. We heard no more on the question of my experience, which was a relief, but the focus was now on the employer's willingness to make the necessary changes at the Mill. The Advocate claimed that his client had experienced real problems in securing the services of a competent engineer to fabricate the necessary fencing round dangerous moving parts of the machinery. He also claimed that in principle his client had no special difficulty with findings of the inspection report, although it was possible to quarrel with one or two aspects. The real difficulty was the problem of implementation and the time that was needed to do this had to be recognised. The Magistrate then asked if the prosecution wished to comment on this to which I replied that I found it difficult to accept the proposition that there had not been adequate time to affect the necessary changes. The need for essential safety measures was long standing as my Report and earlier reports made clear. This request for additional time needs to be judged against the assurances I had received in the past that the matter would be put right forthwith but in reality no action had been taken. It was for this reason that I had found it necessary to resort to Court action.

The Defence Counsel then intervened by submitting that he understood that it was in the Courts powers to make an Order against the Defendant requiring him to comply with the law in a prescribed time.

He suggested that if his client was served with such a Court Order there could be no question as to what his client should do. He went on to say that by setting a time scale in such an Order the matter could be resolved to the Court's satisfaction and this case could now be brought to a close. The Magistrate replied that the desirability of making an Order was essentially a matter for the Court's discretion but he would first welcome the views of the prosecution. The last thing I wanted was for the case to be settled simply on the basis of a Court Order and this proposition was a clever stunt by the Defence Counsel to avoid convictions. This would send completely the wrong signal to other employers in whose premises offences under the Factories Act were evident. If they thought that the only sanction they would face was a possible Court Order then the prospects for getting the necessary improvements to workers safety, health and welfare, would be as far away as ever.

I replied that the defence appeared to be proposing an outcome to the charges on which this prosecution was based designed entirely to suit its own convenience. I pointed out that in putting forward proposals for correcting the offences listed in my Report the defence is admitting the existence of these offences and such an admission can only be taken as a plea of guilty in respect of the offences as charged. The Court's response to such an admission of guilt, and the sanctions that it may decide to impose, are obviously a matter for the Courts own judgement. The prosecution submits that in making its judgement on these offences against the provisions of the Factories Act appropriate sanctions will be reflected in whatever sentence the Court decides to impose. The Court will not need reminding that Factories legislation is designed to ensure that proper regard for the safety, health and welfare, of workers is given by employers. It is the prosecutions view that, where offences under the Act have been identified and brought formally to the attention of the employer concerned and, as in this case, the employer has chosen to persistently ignore the findings and recommendations of an Inspector then on conviction appropriate sentences should be imposed. To do otherwise would be to send the wrong signal to other employers who have responsibilities under the Factories Act. If in addition to the imposition of such sentences the Court in its discretion should also impose a time bound Court Order this would certainly be welcomed by the prosecution.

At this point the Magistrate adjourned the Court for 30 minutes and I received a note from the Court Clerk requesting me to see the Magistrate in Chambers. The Magistrate asked me to clarify my remark about the Court sending the wrong signal to other employers. I explained that contraventions of the Factories Act were a common place in most employing concerns in Dodoma and throughout the Province. I also explained that I had deliberately chosen to prosecute the two major employing concerns in Dodoma both of whom were well able to afford fines if these were imposed. The Court was full of other employers whose attitudes towards safety, health and welfare would be influenced by the out come of these cases If the offender had fines imposed against them there would be a significant change for the better but if the outcome was only a Court Order then in my view there would be little point in me or anyone else trying to enforce the Factories Act.

At the resumption of proceedings the Magistrate very briskly read through the four charges, found the Defendant guilty on all four and imposed a fine of Shgs. 5,000 on each count. He also imposed a Court Order directing compliance within 14 days. I couldn't believe it – nor could the Asians in the court who seemed stunned at the outcome. Fifteen minutes later the case against Mr.Singh was heard. After the charges were read and the accused asked to plead the Defendant, who had sat through the Rice and Oil Mill Case, pleaded guilty as charged. He was fined Shgs. 5,000 on two counts and a Court Order was given requiring compliance within 14 days. Probably due to tension the strain of the previous case I was really feeling tired and was inclined to ask for an adjournment until the next day in respect of the remaining Child Labour case. However, the Defence Counsel claimed that he had urgent business elsewhere and it was agreed to proceed with it forthwith. This case proceeded at a fairly brisk pace the only evidence for the defence was a diatribe from Counsel as to the difficulty employers faced in trying to determine the age of a young worker. His reaction to the medical evidence given by my expert witness was to cross examine him on the reliability of the X-ray. He asked the Doctor if he had ever known a case in which the bones had joined before the age of 12 years. To the Doctors reply of 'Not in my experience' he responded by slapping the X-ray down on the desk of the Court Clerk and shouting 'Well, I have'. Fortunately this didn't convince the Magistrate although it almost convinced me. The Advocate then focussed on the fact that this was the first time that the Defendant had been accused of employing child labour and he assured the Court that this would not be repeated. In the absence of any other substantive evidence the Defendant was found guilty as charged and fined Shgs.3,000.with costs.

It was now 5.30pm and it had been a trying and worrying day the outcome and uncertainty of which I had been worrying about for some time. Back at the Department all the staff were still there and in a pretty cheerful mood, particularly Maloda who took the view that anything that gave the Wahindi a battering was probably a good thing. Aron was fully recovered from his sickness and I was able to congratulate him on his impressive performance. I was also able to thank the Asian doctor and assure him that his costs were now secure. I was surprised at the sense of success on the part of the Messengers who could scarcely have comprehended the details of the cases as they unfolded but they seemed to have a clear understanding of the outcome. I was also surprised to see Mr. Singh waiting to speak to me about something. Without any kind of rancour or complaint he wanted to let me know that not only would he fence his machinery but he was available to do the same for any other employer and perhaps I would be good enough to pass on this message. I had to admire his commercial acumen as, through such arrangements, he doubtless would be able to meet the cost of his fines and still make a profit. In the light of all the good will that seemed to be around I announced that the following day would be a holiday which was certainly welcome except that Panjawani proposed to open the office but take a day off later.

The next morning I went in to the Department at a slightly later time than usual to find Panjawani busy on the telephone. He explained later that he had already had calls from three employers asking for copies of the Inspection Reports on their premises with a view to putting matters right. He said he had expected this and thought that there would be other similar calls during the day. In discussing the court cases I said that I thought that the outcome was well worth the trouble but I wondered how the Defence Advocate had learned about my limited experience and the fact that I had still to pass my law exams. Panjawani with a shrug of his shoulder replied, perhaps a little too swiftly, 'The Staff List'.

PROBLEMS WITH GIFTS

We had now been in Dodoma for almost six months and with the Court cases out of the way now was a good time to take stock of the situation. On the home front we had settled in to our new life style fairly well and we were all enjoying it. Wyn was now confident in dealing with the servants and had mastered enough Swahili to establish a good working relationship although, from time to time, surprises still materialised. The children were settled in the local school and Margaret was doing well although the school itself was quite different to what she was used to. Peter had made a good recovery from his operation without complications which was a great relief and Philip was fine although he was unlikely to pick up another scorpion after his nearly disastrous experience of a sting. So far as the work was concerned things seemed to be going pretty well but of course I was still learning. I had reorganised the Department so that the filing system, formerly the private domain of Panjawani, was now understood and accessible to all of the staff. The place had been thoroughly cleaned and with the help of the Agricultural Department a formal garden had been established on the sandy wasteland in front of the Office. Trees had been planted at the side of the office to provide shade and benches to sit on for people, usually complainants, visiting the Department. Progress with my Swahili was more or less satisfactory but my vocabulary was still too limited. I was benefiting from a sort of tutorial from the Resident Magistrate which was really helpful as I still had my law exam to face. Relations with the staff seemed to be satisfactory but I suppose that we were still getting used to each others peculiarities.

Financially we were just about breaking even and I could now understand why people at my interview board had assumed that I had some sort of private income. My salary which at the point of recruitment seemed fairly generous proved to be just about adequate but we had to draw on savings to get ourselves and the house properly established. Cost of living was going to be a problem and with this in mind Wyn, having got the house and servants sorted out and the children settled, was able to take up a part time teaching assignment at the local Aga Khan School. I was on a salary scale which provided for modest yearly increments but promotion to a higher grade seemed to be the only hope for the future. Our social life centred mainly round the family but Wyn had made friends with our European neighbours mostly through being invited to coffee mornings where she met the wives of other officials. We had also been invited to the 'Club' an institution peculiar to the Colonial Service overseas although private sector members were also allowed to join. The Club operated on the basis of subscriptions from members and was strictly segregated, Africans or Asians were prohibited a rule which was strictly observed. A tennis court and a primitive 9 hole golf course were available and playing a snake did not count as a stroke on the later. Apart from the bar, there was sometimes the possibility of getting a curry lunch at weekends and social evenings such as a dance were organised on a fairly regular basis. I did not feel particularly drawn to this in the first instance and though friends were kind enough to invite us from time to time. Such invitations were frequently refused so as not to give the impression that we were taking advantage of facilities for which other people had to pay a subscription. Certainly the Club provided a useful social purpose and as a place to relax with friends over a drink was a welcome break from the daily routine. The ambience of the Club often depended upon the social range of the members which was fairly wide. At one end of the spectrum was the Provincial Commissioner and senior members of the Administration, then a fair mix of professionals, geologist, surveyors, engineers, vets etc.and towards the other end police inspectors, road foremen, railway mechanics and train drivers. Visiting guests usually included commercial travellers enjoying reciprocity on the basis of club membership elsewhere and technicians on road or dam construction projects out in the bush. The middle group seemed to concentrate on golf and tennis where competitions and trophies were taken very seriously. The last group seemed to concentrate on serious drinking and claimed, with some justification, that it was their efforts at the bar which kept the Club in profit; it was from these people that problems and scandals were likely to arise. One of these, a Charge Nurse at the local Hospital had taken to inviting some Italian road construction workers with whom he, and particularly his wife, had become friendly. They quickly established a reputation for mopping up any spare women about the place – sometimes the wives of officers on safari – and an invitation to their Road Camp was a guarantee of, amongst other things, an ample supply of Italian wine. Why such a woman would choose to put at risk a stable marriage for a questionable relationship with Italians whose usual round the clock companions were local African women, was difficult to comprehend. Inevitably this gave rise to comment and the situation came to a head late one night at the Club when a Road Foreman, with the same surname as myself, rather drunkenly questioned why Italians, who he had fought against during the war, should be allowed in the Club. In the fisticuffs that followed it seems that the drunken Foreman came off worst. I didn't know anything about this until people asked me what on earth I thought I was doing fighting in the Club and as to whether the Committee would be likely to seek an apology. Its one thing to have a reputation as a drunken bruiser, though ill deserved, but to be classified as a failed drunken bruiser was something I could really do without.

A more pressing problem was the need for private transport. As I was not allowed to use the Department's truck for domestic purposes. Colonial Service Regulations made provision for officers such as myself to take out a car loan with repayments being deducted from salary. An incentive to take out such a loan was the possibility of claiming a mileage allowance when using a private car when on safari. Some officers went into the higher calculus trying to work out where the advantage really lay in using Government or private transport. Did mileage allowance really compensate for expenditure on petrol, tax, insurance, maintenance, depreciation, spares and repayments on the car loan etc? The consensus seemed to be that Government came out of the arrangement at the expense of the Officer. I discussed the pros and cons of this with Panjawani who had detailed knowledge of Government General Orders which regulated the conditions under which car loans were granted. Shortly afterwards, doubtless tipped off by Panjawani, three Asians called at the office inviting me to look at a car they claimed had just come on the market. On examination it turned out to be a seven year old Moris Oxford with a mileage of 36,000 and a repainted body. On a test drive the car performed as might be expected for a vehicle of that age and the shock absorbers, brakes and engine were no better than one might anticipate. It was claimed that the former owner was an Indian now in Dar es Salaam and apparently untraceable.

From the familys view point a car was highly desirable since we could drive out into the country side at weekends and even drive some 40 miles to Kongwa where there was a swimming pool. It was also an advantage at night when we were asked out to dinner. Walking in the dark was not without its hazards as snakes and scorpions came out on to the roads, which were still warm even after sunset, and were difficult to spot even with a torch. Hyenas and the possibility of running into a leopard had also to be kept in mind. The Indians who seemed to own the car jointly kept up the pressure on me to buy it and eventually I applied for a Government car loan. They must have been aware of this and were constantly calling round to see if I would agree to buy. This persistence became a nuisance and in some frustration I told them to leave me alone as I had as yet to get my car loan approved by the authorities in Dar es Salaam. I was astonished to receive the reply, 'No, Bwana, your loan has already been approved and the money is in your bank account.' I was learning fast that in Dodoma nothing is really confidential not even in Government service. However, until now I had at least expected to find that my private account at the bank was secure. I called the bank to confirm that my loan had been paid in and then started to haggle on price of the car with the Indians. I was really wasting my time as they knew to a penny how much I had in the bank and the amount of my car loan. I insisted that the car be taken to the Public Works Department so that it could be put up on the ramp and I could inspect the underside. They didn't like this at all but from what I could see the transmission, gear box, differential and brake system seemed to be alright apart from slightly leaking gaskets. I could also see that at some stage the car had been painted red and the subsequent black re-spray had not completely covered the old paint. This raised the doubt in my mind that the car may have been stolen so I asked the local police to check to see if a red car with the same registration number was on the stolen car list. This again caused some consternation amongst the three Indians and two of them seem to fall out of the negotiations at this point. However, I eventually got the message 'nothing known' from the police and we finally agreed a price. I deferred a decision on whether to surrender the Government truck and its driver and use my own car on safaris until I could see how well the car performed.

Just as I had been learning how to work with Africans Wyn was now involved in understanding Asian, particularly Ismaili, culture in connection with her work at the school. The Ismaili community was well established in Dodoma and in addition to building their own school and operating a housing project they had embarked on the construction of a modern Jamat Khama in the centre of the town. This was an impressive project, the largest building in Dodoma, next to the Boma, It was a multi-purpose building serving as a religious centre, a community and health centre and providing a home for an active social welfare programme. Like most Ismaili projects financial assistance had been obtained from the Ismaili's spiritual leader the Aga Khan to whom all Ismailis contributed part of their income on a regular basis. Working mostly with young Asian girls turned out to be a fascinating experience particularly when topics of general interest were under discussion. Shortly after taking up her post as teacher Wyn was asked, in one of these sessions, whether English people were born believing that they were better than everybody else, or whether they were taught this in school. A good if surprising question which made us both think carefully about our general attitude. Towards the end of term when examinations were about to be held Wyn received a number of assurances from various children that if they were given good marks their fathers would give Wyn a good Zawadi – present. Whether this was a straight forward attempt at bribery or simply a way of saying that the present would come by way of thanks for Wyn's teaching abilities was something we could only ponder over.

Our concern about how to detect the line between good-natured generosity and a crude attempt at bribery was severely tested at Christmas. I had set out early on Christmas morning to see if I could shoot some guineafowl hoping we could make Christmas lunch a little more traditional and had taken the dog along with me. On my return I was astonished to find the veranda loaded with presents of every description – bottles of wine, boxes of chocolate, whisky, gin, beer, eggs, samozas, fruit, dates, even cigarettes, although neither of us smoked. Wyn explained that I had no sooner gone than different cars driven by unknown Asians had rolled up the drive and people had deposited the stuff with many Salaams and disappeared. We were totally nonplussed not only by the amount of stuff but the fact that the names on the gifts were simply from Ali, Remtulla, Chandu, et-al, or in some cases no card at all. I was aware of course that as a Government officer I should avoid situations where I might be seen as accepting unwarranted gifts from the local people which might be interpreted as bribes for services rendered. But in this situation I clearly needed some guidance for example were the rules relaxed at Christmas? After some thought I rang the Provincial Commissioner, explained what had happened and asked what I was expected to do. His relaxed response was that these things can happen at Christmas but the best thing is to send the lot back with thanks. Almost as an afterthought he suggested that I might keep the beer.

Returning most of it would not be an easy matter in view of the difficulty of deciding where the stuff had come from in the first place. As all the gifts had been delivered by Asians my only hope was Pajawani so I rang him to explain what had happened. His first reaction was that he couldn't see the problem – why not keep the stuff? I then had to try and explain to him the difficulty re accepting bribes. This was a concept that Panjawani found really hard to grasp and he gave me the impression that he thought that I had gone out of my mind. In the event he agreed to pass the message to his Asian contacts and later in the day various people called to collect the stuff. Wyn had prepared suitable notes expressing grateful thanks to attach to each item. The bleak looks of the children and the servants as all these attractive gifts gradually disappeared was perhaps the worst aspect of the whole experience. It didn't help much to learn subsequently that some of my colleagues in the Administration had taken a much more cavalier attitude in response to something similar but on a smaller scale. When, after Christmas, I discussed the extent of these gifts with Panjawani and asked him why, he explained it simply in two words 'The Prosecutions'.

H.H. PRINCE ALI KHAN

The Ismaili community were astonished to learn that Prince Ali Khan had agreed to visit Dodoma and perform the opening ceremony planned for the newly built School and the recently built Jamat Khama. The leaders of the community had been working on the arrangements for the formal opening for some months, not least because it was an impressive building project of which they could be justifiably proud. A substantial part of the finance necessary to undertake such an ambitious project had been contributed by the local Ismaili community, in particular some of the town's wealthiest commercial business men. In addition, there had been a generous matching grant from the spiritual Leader of the Ismaili's the Aga Khan. Someone had the thought that they might invite the Aga Khan to honour them by agreeing to formally open the Jamat Khama even though it was accepted that a positive response would be extremely unlikely. Against this background they were astonished to receive a formal response indicating that Prince Ali Khan would be delighted to be present on such an auspicious occasion.

The first reaction on hearing of the planned visit of Ali Khan was one of disbelief since the implications were really astonishing. The Aga Khan was not only the spiritual leader of all Ismaili's the world over he was accepted as the persona of God himself and the spiritual blessings that could be derived from simply being in his presence were almost beyond calculation. That his son should make a personal visit to Dodoma changed everything. What was originally planned as a rather formal small scale opening ceremony of Provincial significance was suddenly to be expanded on to a huge National scale with exciting possibilities. Invitations would have be extended to the Ismaili spiritual leaders and other dignitaries in Dar es Salaam and other important Townships throughout the Territory. The new building would have to be illuminated overall and flood lights arranged on the scale of a Sonet Lumiere. Special consideration would have to be given to the catering arrangements in the sense that where refreshments had been planned nothing short of a banquet would now suffice. The Town's accommodation would have to be reviewed and the main Railway Hotel reserved exclusively for His Highness and his entourage. Honoured guests would have to be found accommodation in the residences of the wealthy local members of the Ismaili community and marquees, tents, and a band hired for the various celebrations and social events. Security would become an important issue and the police would have to be consulted in connection with the protection of His Highness and the safety of distinguished guests, but also to prevent gate-crashers at the various events.

Such a visit caught the interest and imagination of the local expatriate community whose knowledge of and interest in Prince Ali Khan reached well beyond his religious persona. For some years the private and social life of Ali Khan had been the focus of the European and American media. His reputation as an extremely wealthy international social celebrity was well established. He was seen by many as the play-boy of the Western World whose exploits in the Casinos, Race Tracks, Ski Resorts and major social events, in the richest cities of the world were seldom out of the headlines. More recently attention had been focussed on his various liaisons with the worlds most beautiful women, the latest of whom was the celebrated film star Rita Hayworth who also enjoyed a headline grabbing reputation in her own right. So far as the Dodoma expatriate community was concerned the visit of Ali Khan was likely to be the most significant social event in years and competition for invitations, particularly amongst the ladies, was almost at fever pitch.

Amongst the various events planned was a visit by His Highness to the Ismaili School, where Wyn was teaching and whose children would feature in the various celebrations. Wyn of course was deeply involved in all this and as a consequence would be formally introduced to the Aga Khan at some point in the proceedings. This gave rise to envious comments from her lady friends who had heard so much of Ali's charm and amazing personality which apparently made him irresistible. Because of Wyn, and against all the odds, given that I was sometimes obliged to chase Ismaili employers, I too received an invitation and I was able to watch events at close range. The reception of His Highness and the formal opening ceremony was an impressive combination of deeply religious and celebratory significance. After various speeches by leaders and clerics of the Ismaili community Ali Khan responded with a carefully thought out speech aimed at consolidating the religious significance of the event combined with warmest congratulations to the Ismaili community as a whole for their magnificent community effort in building the Jamat Khama.

At an appropriate moment a large solid gold key, resting on a velvet cushion, was presented to His Highness who was then invited to open the main door of the Jamat Khama. This was followed by a reception at which various Ismaili dignitaries were formally presented to His Highness. At this point soft drinks were made available and a rather moving scene developed as Ali Khan sipped through a straw at his coca-cola and passed it on to an elderly man stood next to him. He repeated this a number of times to gasps of delight and reverence from the favoured recipients whose reactions to these priceless gifts had to be seen to be believed. At one point His Highness was introduced to a senior Ismaili business man who it was said had made a very generous contribution to the cost of the Jamat Khama. Ali Khan with a charming smile quietly embraced him and the business man (not known to me as a considerate employer) broke down into tears gasping 'You are embracing me' it was as though God had granted him an assurance of direct entry to paradise. This level of reverence seemed to reach out to every one present who seemed to feel that they were in the presence of a spiritual leader of God like significance. Eventually, Wyn was formally introduced and, although a coca cola bottle was not on offer, a warm hand shake and the world famous smile immediately convinced her that Rita Hayworth certainly knew what she was doing and had to be envied. I watched this performance with great interest but my own assessment of the warm professional smile he gave her seemed to convey the hidden message on the lines 'Sod this lot, only you and I really matter and we could become really good friends given the opportunity'. I suspect that it was on his ability to convey something like this in a warm friendly glance to practically any woman, plus the fact that he was enormously wealthy, that his reputation with the ladies was probably based. On the face of it, he looked very similar to many other Asian men in the local community in the same age group. Mid forties, balding, average size and height if slightly overweight, and a pleasant open expression. What made the difference was an air of confidence and assurance typical of people who have enjoyed a good liberal education, good health and the independence generated by immense financial and social security.

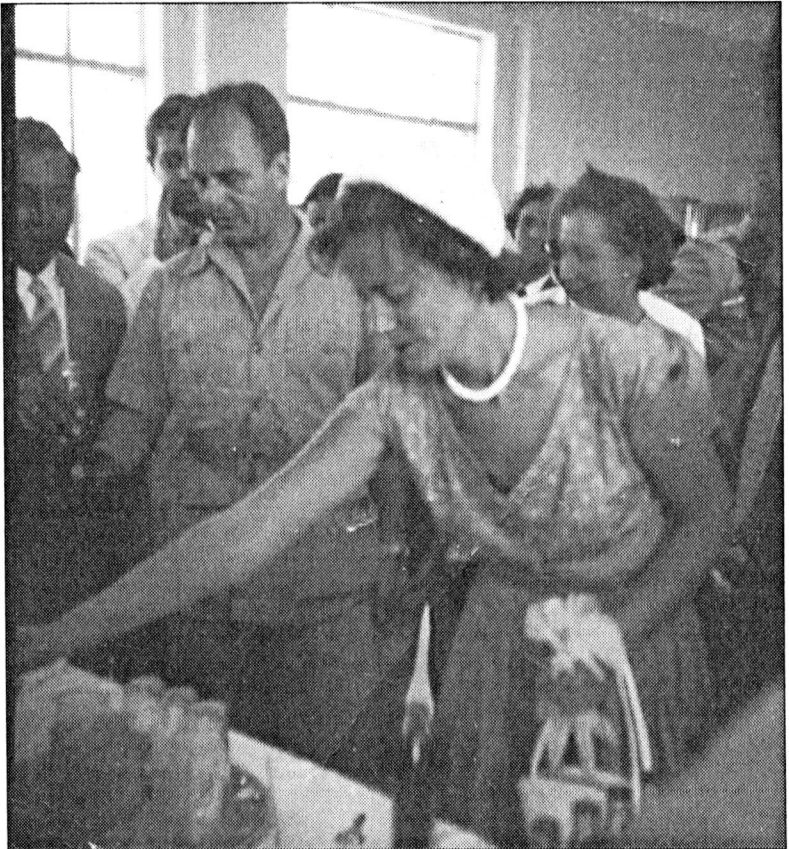

Wyn in the foreground with H.H. Ali Khan

Some time later I was discussing these events with Panjawani who as a practising Hindu seemed to take a jaundiced view of the whole proceedings. He was quick to point out that the Aga Khan had not relinquished the Gold Key but had taken it with him on his departure. He also repeated the rumours circulating in the bazaar that some of the cheques presented in response to the Ismailis' appeal for funds had bounced before the Aga Khan had even departed.

Part 7

SAFARI TO LUFUSI

Walmer and Gruner were Swiss and Swedish entrepreneurs who had prospected for years over many parts of Tanganyika but with singularly little success. Between them they had established an unenviable reputation for failure to repay bank loans, private investors and especially local labour forces engaged in their various enterprises. Notwithstanding their uncertain record they had recently managed to secure a prospecting licence for copper ore and claimed to have found mineable outcrops in the remote Lufusi area just inside the eastern border of the Central Province. There was no record of their operations in the files of the Department and the only evidence of their activities manifested itself in their often-inebriated presence as guests at the Dodoma Railway Hotel. These infrequent visits, lasting only a few days, were reputed to be financed from the proceeds of a delivery of copper ore shipped by rail from Gulwe on the Central line to their agent in Dar es Salaam. Payments for these were made by arrangement through the bank in Dodoma. When such payments were due all work stopped at the mine, Walmer and Gruner presented themselves at the bank and financed by whatever cash was available, a short term fiesta was then set in progress. Little seemed to be known about their residence status but the authorities at the Geological Survey Department seemed to think that they possessed impeccable qualifications as Geologist and Mining Engineer respectively. Their short stays at the hotel followed a predictable pattern, long sessions at the bar before lunch, a steady input of alcohol during lunch, and further drinking after lunch until they were almost falling down drunk at which point they retired to their rooms for a siesta. About six o-clock in the evening they would change for dinner and could be found in the bar and dining room sporting black tie and dinner jackets which had obviously seen punishing service over 30 or 40 years in the tropics.

Frank Glynn

Whatever state of intoxication they achieved, they were always polite and well mannered, especially if ladies were present, and on the face of it caused no trouble to anyone. The Manager of the hotel regarded them as good customers, always able to pay their bills, although it was rumoured that, from time to time, he was obliged to flush noisy African ladies from their bedrooms late in the night. It was against this background that the District Commissioner asked if I would look into the affairs of Walmer and Gruner since he had heard something about unrest in the labour lines at the mine; probably due to unpaid wages. I agreed to carry out an inspection although there was no mining project registered in the Department's files and there was considerable uncertainty as to its exact location, in particular whether it was inside or outside the Province. Since it was known that the copper ore was loaded on to the train at Gulwe and must have been transported by truck or tractor and trailer it would not be difficult to pick up the trail at Gulwe and follow it out to the mine. Discussing the proposed safari with Panjawani he mentioned that some Asian traders had accounts with Gruner and Walmer for the supply of tractor fuel, tools and stores, some of which remained to be settled. Lufusi was not shown on the map but it was thought to be about 70 miles into the bush south of the Central line below Gulwe Station. No road or tracks were shown on the map and the Agricultural and Veterinary officers had no knowledge of mining operations in that area. As usual with any safari Maloda claimed to have been to Lufusi with Bwana Robson-Gibson, a former Labour Officer, but this was treated with derision by Panjawani, Aron and Abdullah the driver. It did not seem to be a difficult safari, since the road to Gulwe was part of the main East / West Road across the Territory and should be in fairly reasonable condition. The tricky bit would be finding the track through the bush south of Gulwe and then keeping on it as it wound up the lower slopes of the Uluguru Mountains where it was thought the mine was located. Provided a start was made at first light it was reasonable to assume that the whole trip could be completed in a day even if this meant returning in the dark. So, preparations were made on that basis with a full tank and two Jerrycans of petrol to be on the safe side. Leaving Dodoma at six in the morning was always a refreshing experience, in bright sunshine but with the heat still to come we made reasonably good progress to Kongwa the former Headquarters of the ill fated Ground Nut Scheme.

With a remarkable indifference to costs the then Labour Government embarked on a major development project designed to grow ground nuts in Tanganyika so as to provide edible oils and fats (margarine) to make up for serious post war shortages. Five thousand square miles of the African bush in the Central and Southern Provinces were to be cleared by fleets of heavy earth moving equipment, operated by a massive expatriate and local labour force. The aim was to create 30,000 acre farms which, ultimately, would be handed over to local Africans within a co-operative system yet to be designed. The British Government Mission despatched to Tanganyika to investigate the proposals for intensive mechanised ground nut production, was influenced by a local South African farmer, who was growing vegetables and maize on a modest scale on his farm at Mpapwa some twenty miles from the small African village of Kongwa. His farm was sited under a line of hills above the Ugogo plain and thus enjoyed modest rainfall, in sharp contrast to the rest of the Central Province. The South African farmer's success depended upon the effective use of furrows he had installed which supplied water (the ownership of which was under litigation) to various parts of the farm. His assurances that groundnut production was a realistic possibility seemed to be the only evidence available to compensate for the complete absence of rainfall statistics.

The Mission accepted his advice even though it must have been obvious that he had a powerful interest in having a major consumer for all his farm produce on the edge of his property. The Mission's Report envisaged that 600,000 tons of ground nuts could be grown at a cost of £14 per ton, compared with world prices of £23, i.e. a saving of £500,000 per annum. The capital costs over six years were estimated at £24 million, including £5.7 million to be spent on heavy agricultural machinery. In the event all these figures turned out to be nonsense – not least because no studies had been made of rainfall or soil analysis and the whole project was launched without troubling to run a pilot scheme.

The Wagogo tribe whose land was to be swallowed up in the scheme and who had centuries of experience of the land's potential were not consulted; its ironic that the word 'Kongwa' (where the Scheme's Headquarters were to be established) in Chi-Gogo means 'a delusion'. It turned out that only 150,000 acres were in fact cleared (target 600,000) at a cost of £40 to£50 per acre instead of the estimated £4 and that the overall expenditure was £11,000,000 over budget. After three years it was obvious that the Scheme had failed in its primary objective, to grow ground nuts, and it was generally accepted that something in the order of £25,000,000 had probably been lost.

In the Central Province, five years after the collapse of the Project, all that was left was a collection of wooden huts at Kongwa now used as a temporary boarding school with an uncertain future. The bush has now re-established itself over the cleared land and the game and wild life are now back in their former habitat. So too are the Wagogo, back in their tribal lands practicing 'slash and burn' type traditional agriculture and, subject to rainfall and their unique planting system, growing small harvest of ground nuts. The old wooden buildings scattered widely across the scheme hold no attractions for them and they have rebuilt their traditional housing of mud and wattle and using the huts as cattle bomas or for small stock, but more often for 'kuni' – firewood. We were driving along the northern trace of the ground nut scheme on what was probably the longest and straightest road in the Territory; 35 miles across the Ugogo plain without a diversion of any kind and now hemmed in by the bush on either side. Maloda was moved to comment that 'If a man had to walk this road he would surely think that God had forgotten him'.

Arriving at Gulwe, a small station where the Central line trains took on water and fuel, the place seemed deserted and since no train was expected the Asian Station Master was missing. Checking at the local 'duka' we were told that no petrol was available and with advice from a Sergeant at the Police Post we found the track leading out of Gulwe in the direction of the mine. He claimed not to have heard of any trouble at the mine which he pointed out was not in his District. He also seemed to think that ore from the mine was now being transported by tractor and trailer on a road which had been opened up on the edge of the Uluguru mountains leading to Morogoro station in the Eastern Province. Asked why Gulwe was so deserted he explained that the Overseer / Dresser from the clinic in Kilosa had arrived to carry out a vaccination programme designed to deal with a local outbreak of small pox – the people were afraid of the 'sindano' – vaccination needle.

Gulwe is a weary sort of place even when trains are due and I was reminded of a recent scandal concerning two people stationed at the Cattle Research Station at Mpapwa where a small community of expatriates were based some twenty miles north of Gulwe. It seems that a couple, who were both married, had convinced themselves that they were in love and in some desperation planned to elope to Dar es Salaam. They quietly left Mpapwa during a Saturday night dance at the local Club, using a truck borrowed from the Veterinary Department, with a view to boarding a train scheduled to leave Gulwe station at mid-night. However their absence was spotted late in the evening and a somewhat inebriated convoy, including their respective spouse, decided to seek them out rightly assuming that they must have left for Gulwe. As is often the case, the train was late and by the time the search party from the Club arrived, the two absconders were waiting forlornly on the station platform. The subsequent embarrassment and recriminations can be imagined, however, life returned to normal fairly quickly and the whole experience put down to alcohol, boredom and 'Bloody Africa'. A common enough defense for all manner of social stupidities.

In the absence of any petrol at Gulwe we had nearly three quarters of a tank and two jerrycans in reserve so it was calculated we could complete the 70 miles or so out to the mine and return without any special difficulty. The real problem would be the state of the track which would doubtless have sustained some damage during the recent rains. However, if it was possible to get a tractor and trailer loaded with copper ore from the mine to Gulwe I did not anticipate any particular

difficulties. The safari team on this occasion was limited to
Abdullah, Aron and Maloda as we were not expecting an
overnight stay. The land south of Gulwe was typical of most of
Ugogo, semi-desert thorn scrub interspersed with acacia and
miombo trees with a fair number of good sized Baobabs and
uphobia cactus like bushes. The first 30 miles were covered
without incident although the pace was slow due to the very poor
state of the track, wash-a-ways having to be filled in at fairly
frequent intervals. We passed old Gogo 'tembes' in fairly isolated
locations but there were very few people in evidence. There was
no sign of game of any sort although Maloda kept a pretty sharp
lookout and although there was a rich variety of bird life there
was nothing worth shooting.

Our problems started when we reached a break in the track
where the trail split into three separate directions none of which
were signed. There were no shambas about where we might have
made inquiries so the decision which track to take had to be a
matter of guess work. Since we could see the Uluguru Mountain
range in the far distance to the south east and it was conjectured
that the Lufusi mine would be in the foothills at the western edge
I decided that we should follow the track leading in that direction.
Four miles farther on, the track deteriorated rapidly and speed
had to be reduced to about 12 miles an hour, due to the pot-holed
and rocky surface, with consequent high petrol consumption. We
had to stop when we came across a deep but dry 'Karonga' the
wooden bridge over which had completely collapsed. Judging
from the state of the timber supports it was obvious that the
bridge had been out of action for years and most of the wood had
been eaten away by white ants. It was inconceivable that we
might re-build it to a state where it would safely support the
weight of the truck. It also became clear that it would not be
possible to find a diversion round the bridge because of the steep
banks of the karonga. Amongst the bits of wood that had not been
washed away was a scarcely legible Notice warning that the bridge
was unsafe.

There was no alternative but to return back to the junction and
then try one of the remaining two options, neither of which looked

particularly promising. We chose the one leading more or less in a southerly direction and after about five miles the scrub-land changed into more open country with quite a few large ant hills scattered about; some reaching a height of 15 or 16 feet. It was Maloda's firm conviction that the larger of these would invariably be the home of a Black Mamba – the bigger the ant hill the bigger the snake. So far as wildlife was concerned things seemed to be pretty quiet – the bird life was confined to cape doves and the odd horn-bill but there was no evidence of people, not even deserted shambas or any sign of 'slash and burn' type clearings. Commenting on the absence of people Aron seemed to think that that they had moved out of the plain up into the Uluguru's to avoid malaria and to escape sleeping sickness from the tsetse flies which were now becoming a nuisance.

Eventually the red laterite soil changed to black cotton soil and there were indications that the land would change into marsh during the rainy season. For the first time we found some evidence that a tractor or heavy vehicle had been along the track and we were speculating as to whether this was mine traffic or perhaps Asian traders collecting charcoal from burners scattered throughout the area. Again, because of the poor condition of the track, we were only averaging about 10 or 12 miles an hour and even then the truck's suspension was taking a battering. I estimated that Lufusi could only be about another 40 miles and unless the road improved it seemed likely that we would have to spend the night at the mine. Abdullah was in favour of returning to Gulwe which we could probably reach soon after dark and where, although this wasn't mentioned, there was a small mosque. Whilst we were having a short break to let Aron recover from the singularly bumpy drive we were surprised to see two Africans emerge from the bush on to the track about sixty yards in front of us. They seemed astonished to see us and immediately dashed back into the bush. In view of their odd behavior I walked up the road to make contact and Maloda and Aron followed, the later carrying the gun as though expecting trouble. Just off the track we found a group of four Africans waiting in the bush who were then joined by a European and an Asian. I had the distinct impression that we were most unwelcome but it was not obvious why. The European was a short, thick set, red haired type, about 40 years old, wearing a bush jacket and khaki longs which had certainly seen some action. He was perspiring heavily and gave the impression that he was very annoyed about something. As I approached I called out, 'Good afternoon, I wonder if you could tell me if this is the track to Lufusi?'

'Hello, I don't think I have ever heard of Lufusi but this is not my area. What brings you out here?'

'Oh, I'm the Labour Officer from Dodoma and I believe there is some trouble at the copper mine at Lufusi.'

He then asked his people if they knew anything about Lufusi but no one seemed to have heard of it. I then asked him 'What brings you into this part of the world?' After some hesitation he explained that he was an Agricultural Officer from Morogoro and was carrying out a survey in connection with a re-settlement scheme.

'Have you any idea where this track might lead to?'

'Not really, but I have heard that there is an Italian trying to establish a mixed farm somewhere to the south of here.'

Without another word he then led his party off in to the bush on the opposite side of the track. They were a strange group, not least because although he claimed to be carrying out a survey they did not seem to have any survey equipment, or indeed any safari gear at all. However, they were carrying an impressive battery of guns including a 600 double which could have been a Rigby, a 375 Magnum with a telescopic sight and a double barreled shot gun.

After they had gone I asked Aron what he thought of them.

'There is something very strange about these people – they did not want to be seen for some reason.'

'That was my impression too, but what could they be up to?'

Whilst I had been talking to the Agricultural Officer, Maloda had been speaking in Chigogo to a Mgogo who was in the party. So I asked Maloda what he thought about them.

'Bwana, watu hawa wamepiga tembo – kubwa sana, huko' – 'Sir, these people have shot an elephant, a very big one over there', pointing into the bush with his chin.

Of course this explained everything and just as we were walking back to the truck the Agricultural Officer came back on to the road and asked if he could speak to me privately.

As we walked back towards the truck he said 'I think you should know that the proposed re-settlement project would affect substantial numbers of theWapogoro tribe who would have to be moved and this would be a tricky and difficult operation. It is important that the people who are to be re-settled should not be informed until the project is properly prepared, so it would be best if you would treat our meeting as confidential, in fact as though it never happened.'

'Well, I hear what you say but if the re-settlement issue comes up at the Provincial Security Committee I may well have to mention it if I am asked'. This was clearly not the response he was expecting and he snapped 'this is strictly an Eastern Province matter and you would be wise to keep out of it.' Without further comment he stalked off back into the bush.

The thought occurred to me that one reason for his odd behaviour might be that he had been engaged in unlicensed shooting, otherwise what was all the fuss about. Discussing it with the team it was generally agreed that this must be the case but I was wondering why the Asian would be involved and Aron seemed to think that he would probably buy the meat after the trophies had been removed.

, Of course there was always the possibility that on his return to Morogoro the first thing he would do would be to buy an elephant licence to cover his tracks retrospectively. Such a situation was not all that unusual and to some of the more adventurous officers it offered a partial solution to the problem of childrens school fees. The possibility of shooting a decent sized elephant, with tusks weighing 80 or 90 lbs. a side, provided a risky but welcome financial return on a £20 elephant licence. The key factor was finding a suitable elephant in the first place and this usually required good intelligence, such as a tip off from a Game Scout or local tribesmen. Few people would be willing to take out a £20 licence just on the off chance and face the hazards of taking on a bull elephant unless a suitable target was known to be available without the need for an extensive safari. It was sometimes the case that a good-sized elephant may be encountered by accident and, provided that one was suitably armed and had adequate back-up, there was a great temptation to shoot the absence of a licence notwithstanding. This had to be balanced against the possibility that a poor shot could, and sometimes did, result in the officer being seriously hurt or trampled to death by a wounded and infuriated elephant.

For sensible conservation reasons elephant licences were restricted to two elephants a year per person and for those few individuals seriously interested in big game shooting this limitation proved fairly irksome. A retired Brigadier who ran a small mixed farm on the southern borders of the Province was a keen elephant hunter who devoted a considerable amount of his time to planning and implementing his own elephant shooting safaris. Each year he would carefully select an area in the remoter part of the Southern Province and plan to be away for two to three months with a well equipped team of carefully selected Africans with proven tracking and hunting skills. On one occasion, having planned a safari into the remote region of the Great Ruaha river valley, he set off with his two newly acquired licences. On the evening of the first day he was surprised to encounter a magnificent bull elephant quietly browsing close to the track with tusks judged to be well in excess of 100 lbs each. After deploying his team and carefully stalking he was able to get into close shooting range in good cover; the mythology with elephants is that you must get as close as you possibly can – and then get 10 yards closer. In almost perfect conditions he fired for a brain shot with his 600 double killing cleanly and instantly.

After such a surprising and satisfactory outcome they set up camp with a view to chopping out the tusks and securing the other trophies. This meant keeping fires burning throughout the night to keep off predators and scavengers but the outcome was a good pair of undamaged tusks weighing 106 and 113 lbs respectively.

Within two days he was able to carry on his safari heading farther into the Ruaha valley with the intention of establishing camp at a suitable site on the river bank. From here he planned to carry out a series of extended foot safaris in different directions over the next few weeks. Towards evening as the tents were being erected he walked along the bank with his 12 bore shotgun hoping to shoot duck or guinea fowl for the evening meal. Whilst scouting for birds one of his trackers found warm elephant dung only six hundred yards from the camp and further tracking revealed a magnificent male elephant drinking and sluicing in the shallows on the rivers edge. Both tusks looked to be sound and were estimated to be in excess of 100lbs each. Shooting conditions were almost perfect in the sense that there was no wind, the river bank was clear of bush apart from low scrub and there was sufficient cover to get a close shot as the elephant came back up the bank. Conditions were exceptional, the light was still good and the temptation to shoot was irresistible so the tracker was sent back to the camp to alert the team and bring the rifles. In the meantime the Brigadier was left with the dilemma that if the elephant was shot his licences would be filled and the carefully planned and much anticipated three months safari would be at an end. Within minutes the team and guns had arrived, stalking into selected shooting positions was accomplished without alarming the elephant and as it returned to the bank a single shot knocked the elephant to its knees and a second heart shot effected a clean and easy kill. Notwithstanding the very satisfactory financial outcome, the Brigadier was confronted with the bleak reality that his three months planned safari had fizzled out in less that a week and it would be twelve months before new licences would be available.

About six miles further along the track the thick scrub land changed into more open spaced savannah country with a much clearer view of the Uluguru range of mountains. In the late afternoon some game were evident in the distance including two groups of giraffe and Grants and Thompsons gazelles. Maloda said there must be some water some where in this area although there was no evidence of this but a small stream coming down from the Ulugurus was a possibility. As the road levelled out we came to a trail leading off to the left in an easterly direction and there were faint tracks of a vehicle which had taken a swing to the east along this new trail. After some discussion we continued to follow the track we were on as there was some evidence that a tractor or heavy goods vehicle had recently been using this trail. It was now turned 5.00 o'clock and it would be dark in another hour so we pressed on with all speed hoping to reach the mine or the Italian shamba before sunset.

We were now travelling along the lower slopes of the Ulugurus and over a slight rise we suddenly came across a valley of cleared land with well laid out crops of maize and millet and farm buildings in the distance. Closer to the farm we crossed a small bridge over a well maintained furrow which fed water into the farms irrigation system. Beyond the farm buildings in the distance a collection of grass bandas were established which looked as though they were used as labour lines and fires had been lit ready for the evening meal. As we drove up to the farm buildings we were surrounded by a pack of dogs barking furiously circulating the truck and making it quite clear that we would be at risk if we dismounted. Eventually as the noise continued a rather large, heavily pregnant, middle aged European lady came out on to the veranda and with an impressive stream of Italian and Swahili managed to call off the dogs. Having judged that it was safe to dismount I walked over to the veranda – the others staying nervously in the truck. The lady turned out to be Mrs. Rosa whose husband, also Italian, was out working somewhere in the shamba. Having introduced myself and explained the reason for my presence she confirmed that the two Swiss miners were operating an open cast mine about three miles farther down the valley but she thought that they had probably gone to Morogoro.

Since it was now almost dark she kindly suggested that I should stay the night and visit the mine in the morning. I had to explain that I had three Africans with me and wondered what if any accommodation might be available for them. She thought that they would probably find accommodation at the labour lines where there was a small duka at which they could get something to eat. This seemed to be the only option apart from sleeping in the truck and since I was able to advance their overnight subsistence allowance the team decided to explore the possibilities at the duka. Mrs. Rosa was kind enough to invite them to help themselves to maize cobs from the store and bananas and paw paws from the kitchen garden. It turned out that Mrs Rosa's English was fairly limited but she was comfortable speaking

Swahili and did her best to make me welcome. Having off loaded my gear and the rifle, I told Aron that if he could not find somewhere to sleep he should come back and we would think of something else but if things worked out satisfactorily they should pick me up at 7.00 o'clock next morning.

Shortly after the truck had left Mr. Rosa made a noisy appearance with a tractor and two more dogs. He expressed surprise to find me at the farm explaining that, apart from Gruner and Wolmar, he had not had any visitors apart from a Land Bank official, since he set up the farm. During discussions over drinks before supper he mentioned that he had been granted a ten year lease on the valley from the Custodian of Enemy Property with a licence for mixed farming. In three years he had established the farm buildings using mostly local materials – mainly burnt brick and mud and wattle construction with thatched roofs.

He had developed the furrow bringing surface water from the lower slopes of the Ulugurus sufficient to sustain a reliable irrigation system and using traditional 'slash and burn' methods had cleared enough land to plant maize, millet and some tobacco. At first he relied on local daily paid labour, mostly women, as the men had proved to be unreliable and less productive. Last year he had been able to buy the tractor – an old reject from the ground nut scheme – which he had managed to repair. Against this background, Mrs. Rosa had developed a substantial kitchen garden, growing vegetables, bananas and paw-paw and had goats and fowl providing milk and eggs; her ambition was to grow vines and eventually produce wine.

During conversation over dinner – paw-paw, spaghetti with meat sauce, and banana fritters, I asked what brought them to Tanganyika. It turned out that Rosa who had been employed as a farm labourer in northern Italy had been conscripted into the army during the war and captured by the British in Somalia. He spent the rest of the war in a prison camp in Kenya but was allowed out to do farm labouring in the area of the camp. After the war he couldn't settle in post Mussolini Italy (he was a great supporter Mussolini who he thought made a serious mistake in getting involved with Hitler) and managed to get back to Kenya working as a mechanic, a building and construction worker and eventually manager on a mixed farm in KikuyuLand. He came down to Tanganyika when the Ground Nut scheme started and worked as a tractor driver / mechanic on land clearing until the scheme failed.

After carefully reconnoitring different agricultural possibilities he decided to risk all his savings and a Land Bank loan to develop (gamble on) Lufusi and with sustained hard work, courage and admirable self reliance, had obviously made an impressive start. His major worries centred round the reliability of the water supply, crop raiding by animals and people – he lost a quarter of his maize crop last year due to raids by baboons. This year the problem was stealing by local people so he said don't be surprised if you hear gunshots tonight, if I see lights down the valley I fire a few rounds in that direction to scare off people stealing. Another current problem was leopards, two were raiding the small stock and were after the dogs which was a worry and thus far they had evaded any attempts to trap them. Although it wasn't mentioned there were three very fine leopard skins in the lounge so he had obviously had some success in dealing with this issue.

My bedroom was a small mud and wattle extension to the main building with a thatched roof and earth floor. There was a gap of about a foot between the top of the walls and the roof so there was plenty of ventilation and the bed was a 'kitanda' locally made but with a clean mattress and sheets and a new mosquito net. By nine thirty I was comfortably in bed with the mosquito net securely tucked in and an oil lamp which provided enough light but not enough to read by. However, it was bright enough to attract every creepy crawly in creation. Geckos emerged from the roof thatch and chased about the walls after moths and insects and large hunting spiders ran across the dirt floor in pursuit of anything that moved. This reminded me that scorpions would not be too far away so I put my desert boots inside the net in case I had to visit the outside deep pit latrine during the night.

Having put the lamp out everything seemed pitch black but my eyes soon adjusted to the moonlight coming through the gap between the top of the walls and the roof eaves. Thinking about the team I was fairly confident that they must have found food and accommodation otherwise, knowing them, they would certainly have been back by now to complain. Because of the gap at the top of the walls the usual African night noises seemed much in evidence, crickets, frogs, owls and other night creatures all contributing the racket which is the typical African night. In the distance hyenas were making their presence felt with their unmistakable whooping calls and my last thoughts before dropping off into a deep sleep were of the beautiful leopard skins which adorned the walls of Rosa's sitting room.

I was suddenly awakened by a series of rifle shots being fired about twenty feet away from me which triggered off a cacophony of barking from the dogs in the compound. I then remembered Rosa's warning that this was his method of discouraging people stealing his maize crop and in between the barking of the dogs I thought I could hear cries of alarm in the far distance. Checking my watch it was only 10-30 but it wasn't long before the dogs settled down and I drifted off to sleep again.

I was awakened suddenly by an urgent scratching and scrambling noises outside the mud wall close to my head. Then some creature landed with a thud on to my mosquito net which collapsed and landed on me. In something of a panic I grabbed my torch from under my pillow to discover what was happening. My first thoughts was that it was a leopard but it turned out to be Rosa's cat which had been chased by something outside and escaped through the gap at the top of the wall. After unscrambling itself from the net the cat shot under the bed and stayed there whilst I in some trepidation waited anxiously to see what might follow. In the event nothing else came through and after extricating myself from the mosquito net and connecting it up to the roof again I finally settled down to sleep.

I was up at first light awakened by Rosa starting his tractor and the dogs barking. In the course of breakfast, paw-paw, maize porridge and eggs, we were discussing Mrs. Rosa's impending confinement and it became obvious that no special plans had been made. My concern was the isolation of the farm and the distance and poor road to Mpapwa where the nearest medical help was available. Since this was Mrs. Rosa's first child and I judged her to be about forty years old this seemed to be a pretty worrying situation, particularly if there was the possibility of a premature birth. I suggested that nearer the time of her confinement she should come and stay with us in Dodoma where Wyn could keep an eye on her and good medical help was readily available. This offer was seized upon by both of them with some relief and, in the event, this worked out fine. Mrs. Rosa subsequently stayed with us for about two weeks before giving birth to a fine baby girl without complications.

The team arrived with the truck at 7.00, Maloda who looked as though he was suffering from a pretty fair hangover said he was ngonjwa (sick), but Aaron said he was drunk, otherwise they were in good shape. so we drove off in search of the mine following Rosa's instructions. As mines go it was a sad scene, there was a small primitive open cast mine based on pick and shovel extraction with some evidence of blasting. The labour lines consisted of a few small grass bandas made from local materials and were occupied by a few families-mostly women and children. Water was drawn from the furrow and there was no evidence of any form of sanitation. Eventually the local headman made an appearance who said that most of the men were working on Bwana Rosa's shamba but some had gone looking for meat as they had heard that an elephant had been shot somewhere. Gruner and Walper shared a mud and wattle house some distance from the labour lines and the Headman explained that there was a nominal roll of workers in Bwana Gruner's house but that they had both gone away. Gruner's cook / houseboy was able to produce the roll and a pile of completed 'Kipandis' from which it was possible to get a rough idea of how much the unpaid wage bill might be. In the meantime word had spread of our presence and about thirty men came forward claiming unpaid wages. In the event they accepted that action would be taken to ensure that all oustanding wages would be paid when we could contact Gruner. It was clear from their attitude that delays in paying wages was a more or less common event payment usually being made following a delivery of a load of ore. From the complaints we had received and the Headman's explanation of the nominal roll it looked as though the total outstanding wage bill would not exceed Shgs 8,000.

In the absence of the two engineers it was obvious that little could be done so I left a copy of the Department's Inspection Report form with the Headman with instructions that it be given to Gruner on his return. I left a further copy with Rosa who promised to see that it was served on Gruner as soon as he heard he was back.

The return journey to Dodoma was accomplished without incident, other than two punctures on the same tyre, additional petrol was obtained from the veterinary Department at Mpapwa. Getting a solution to the unpaid wages would depend on a sensible response from Gruner and Walpar. As a precaution, I contacted the Bank Manager at Dodoma so that he would withhold payment of any cash cheque presented by them until I had been informed. In the event this is what happened and it was arranged that Aron would return with them to the mine to ensure payment. They also agreed to provide transport to get Aron back to Gulwe where he could then board a train back to Dodoma.

CAVE PAINTINGS AT KONDOA

During a conversation with a friend, who was a District Officer responsible for the northern area of the Central Province, he mentioned that he had heard that there were pre-historic cave paintings in the Kondoa area and asked if I would be interested in visiting them. Since this only involved a days safari and there would doubtless be a chance to shoot guinea-fowl in the process we arranged to go at the weekend. His information was based on reports he had heard from a local Headman and there was the possibility that we may not find anything. However, it was arranged that a guide should meet us at a suitable point north of Kondoa up the Great North Road and that he would lead us to the site which would involve about an hours foot safari. We left Dodoma early one Sunday morning taking a gun, torches, and a packed lunch; I also decided to take my dog in case we managed to get some shooting.

When we reached the pick up point it turned out that there were three guides, all local Wagogo, who were curious to see what we might find in the cave. It was made clear right at the outset that under no circumstances would they be willing to enter the cave with us. No specific reason was given for this other than a general feeling that the cave was probably haunted by spirits and there was a chance that they would encounter some form of bad luck or become bewitched. There was nothing surprising about this as the Wagogo are notoriously fearful of spirits which may if disturbed cause problems for any intruders. Their interest in the visit was to see at first hand whatever mishap we may encounter as a consequence of entering the cave. We walked through the bush, which was mainly open savannah with Baobab and Acacia trees and scrub bush, until we could see in the distance some rocky outcrops in which the cave was located. As we got nearer the outcrops we could see that they were really very large boulders which looked as though they had been forced up

through the plain by volcanic action These were not unusual in
the Central Province and were the kind of place in which Hyraxes
and Baboons could be found and although there was some
evidence of their presence no actual sightings were made.
Judging from the entrance to the cave it seemed as though this
was formed by two very large boulders leaning against each other
leaving a fairly narrow gap between them.

Since it was now passed midday we found some shade and decided
to have lunch before attempting to make an entrance and we were
both struck by the strange silence. Unusual in the African bush,
as there was no sign of bird life and even the crickets refrained
from making their constant racket. The dog sat close to us
making no attempt to scout about as was normal for him and
although he sniffed carefully at the entrance to the cave he made
no attempt to go in. The guides sat quietly about ten yards away
speculating as to what might be in the cave. Setting aside the
inevitable spirits and 'shetani' the possibility of snakes were
discussed, scorpions most likely, hyenas were not ruled out but
the unspoken question was is there likely to be a leopard and,
worst still will it have cubs? In the event of the later whoever
attempted to go inside would have no chance whatsoever. Against
this background my friend suggested that we might fire a couple
of rounds into the cave as a first step to see what if any reaction
this might provoke. However, the only reaction was from the
Guides all of whom seemed to get ready for instant flight and the
dog crouched down away from the entrance whimpering quietly
unwilling to follow us in. In the event we encountered no
problems, the cave was larger than we had anticipated and the
roof seemed to be about twelve feet high narrowing down to about
four feet at the far end. The floor was fairly level, sandy but
littered with small rocks which must have fallen from the roof
over time but there was no trace of animal spoor other than some
ancient bone fragments which might have been left by hyenas.

As the torch beams swept the smooth north face of the cave some
brownish markings came to light which on close examination
revealed the most detailed sketch of a group of human figures and
above them on either side some small vertical markings made by

single strokes of a brush. The painting which was in brownish red ochre was of quite astonishing artistic merit portraying a dramatic encounter between what seemed to be four male figures and in the centre one female. We half expected to find crude drawings of animals and stick figures representing hunters such as have been found in a number of sites in this part of the Rift Valley but this was completely different. On close examination it was a drawing of a group of five people perhaps performing a dance or, more likely, engaged in some form of dispute. The first thing that struck one was the quality of the drawing and the fact that, although they were only simple stick figures, the effect was grippingly atmospheric. What at first seemed to be a depiction of a dance seemed on further examination to take on a more sinister aspect suggesting that a drama or conflict was being enacted. On one interpretation, it might be seen as a conflict as two men seize the woman and try to draw her away whilst the other two men might be seen as resisting such action. Alternatively, one might equally assume that the people on the right are in the process of giving the female away to the people on the left. The female who is the central feature of the drama appears to be resisting or perhaps dejectedly accepting her fate. All of this is of course pure speculation on my part and the impression the artist was trying to convey remains an enigma open to all kinds of interpretation. My sketch at page 230 offers a fairly accurate depiction of the actual painting but fails to capture its atmosphere.

One can only speculate about the motivation of the artist and what specifically impelled him (or it could, given the subject matter, be her) to paint this astonishing revelation in such an uncertain and possibly dangerous location Does it reflect some uniquely secret ceremony never intended to be viewed by other people? What equipment would be available to the artist in the first place? Red ochre mixed with oil or animal fat seems to be the media but a light of some sort would be necessary possibly a wick in an oil container or a fire, and a brush teased out of a suitable small twig seems likely. A further question arises when consider-ation is given to the 22 small vertical marks above the drawing obviously done at the same time but their significance remains uncertain – an indication of 'bride price' or simply practice brush strokes; who knows? The longer one stares at the painting the more enigmatic it becomes. The question as to when it was painted is perhaps less difficult to answer in the sense that detailed analysis has been carried out by distinguished scientists such as the Leakie family whose work on African pre-history is so impressive. Mary Leakie is known to have actively traced some eighty odd cave paintings at recorded sites in Tanganyika and they have reached the conclusion that such paintings were made 8,000 to 35,000 years ago.

Whenever I think of this particular African rock painting I am reminded of the events which occurred after we left the cave and were walking back to the truck. As we moved through the bush we came across a small group of Wagogo following a track which crossed the path we were trying to follow. The two men at the front were holding a young girl firmly by her arms as if to prevent her from running away. The girl seemed to be about 14 years old and was in a pretty desperate state, crying as if her heart was broken and from the looks of her she had obviously been severely beaten. Behind them was an old man probably in his sixties although these things are hard to judge. He was dirty, toothless, but chewing tobacco, both eyes affected by trachoma and wearing an old goat skin and dirty shuka which had seen better days. He probably hadn't washed since the last rains, his grey hair was matted and his scrawny arms and legs were scaly and dry in line with his generally scrofulous appearance. Behind him were three other younger men. When we stopped and asked what was the problem we were told 'She has refused'. It turned out that the old man had recently married the young girl having paid a generous 'bride price' in cattle to her parents. The girl had found that she couldn't stand it and in desperation had attempted to run away. The implications of this for the family were quite serious in the sense that the cattle had been shared out amongst them and unless the girl could be made to return the bride price would have to be repaid. When I asked my friend if there was anything we might do he pointed out that this was native law and custom and was a matter over which we had no jurisdiction; to interfere would doubtless cause a serious tribal dispute.

Cave painting, N. Kondoa. A copy painted by the author which, sadly, fails to capture the quality of the original or reflect its atmospheric impact.

THE SECURITY COMMITTEE

Having been in my post for almost nine months I was fairly comfortable with my assignment. The office was running smoothly, the inspection programme was under control and the staff seemed to be content and working well. To the extent that I could detect any dissatisfaction this came from Maloda who preferred to be on constant safari. He obviously enjoyed being away from Dodoma and it was Aron's view that Maloda's two wives were a factor in his desire to be away. Moloda had sometimes asked if there was some European medicine to help him better fulfil his marital obligations complaining that 'he could only do two safaris a night'. It crossed my mind that perhaps I should find out what he was taking to support this level of performance. I was constantly busy, partly because there was now a noticeable increase in the number of complaints with workers coming in from as far away as Manyoni or even Singida. So far as industrial relations were concerned, Dodoma was a relatively quiet place as there were only two trade unions of any real consequence, the Railway African Union and the African Civil Servants Staff Association. Both these had very modest paid up memberships, workers usually seeking membership when they were involved in a dispute with their employers. Strike action was sometimes discussed, particularly with the Railway African Union, but disputes were usually settled through conciliation with the help of the Department. The Union's leadership was predominantly Muslim and because of this they had an extensive net work of contacts across the Territory which over-rode tribal boundaries. Abdullah the driver, who was an ardent Muslim, reported that the relative calm amongst railway workers would soon be likely to change. This was because a new General Secretary had been elected in Dar es Salaam, a Mr. Tumbo, who was known to be a militant and likely to cause trouble if only to establish his own leadership credentials.

Frank Glynn

As Provincial Labour Officer, I was automatically a member of the Provincial Security Committee which met monthly at the Boma under the Chairmanship of the Provincial Commissioner. The membership was quite small consisting of the District Commissioner, the Superintendent of Police, who was an elderly, much be-meddled officer who regarded the Committee as pretty much his own preserve. He tried to convey the impression that there was very little of any significance in the Province that he was not already aware of. He also managed to convey the impression that, because of my limited experience, I was unlikely to be of any value to the committee and might, because of my closeness to Africans, even be something of a security risk. Furthermore, he took the view that nothing of any significance was likely to develop on the labour relations front that could possibly interest a high level committee such as this. The remaining member of the committee was a fairly non-discript Arab / Swahili in an embroidered Kofia (cap), and a scruffy long Kanzu reaching down to his sandaled feet, with a deep scar running from his left eye to his mouth only partly hidden by an untidy beard. He remained nameless since no one troubled to introduce him but he was obviously a creature of the Superintendent and was presumably on the police pay-roll. According to my own staff this person was well known in Dodoma and was generally regarded as a local police 'nark'.

I found these meetings interesting, if slightly surreal, so far as I could see no minutes were kept, presumably for security reasons, and the Agenda appeared to be set by the Police Superintendent. Discussions usually focussed on the activities of Asian business men, often referred to as a certain gentleman. Their involvement in such issues as diamond smuggling, cattle theft, and poaching of game trophies were sometimes mentioned but the main interest lay in the activities of Asian visitors to the Province who were suspected of being Marxist activists. Their movements and the names of people they met were reported in detail although what was discussed at such meetings was never mentioned. The District Commissioner would comment on the behavior of local Chiefs and Headmen in the context of tribal politics and, less frequently, murders and tensions in the local communities due to witchcraft. So far a security was concerned it was evident that the major threat from the police viewpoint was the activities and influence of Arabs, Asians and Chinese, who were known to be communists. It seemed likely that the Provincial Police were alerted to the presence of such visitors by the Special Branch Unit in Dar es Salaam with a request that they be kept under surveillance.

I had some difficulty with this since the policy and, to a lesser extent the programmes, designed to advance Tanganyika towards independence were well established at least in principle and the prospects for converting the country into a Marxist State in the short term seemed totally unreal. The terms of the United Nations Mandate were quite clear and the United Kingdom as the Administering Authority was obliged to take account of the recommendations of the U.N. Trusteeship Council Missions which visited the Territory on a regular basis. It was generally accepted that eventually the country would become independent on the basis of free elections and since the majority of people eligible to vote (98%) were Africans they would inevitably come to rule. The crucial issue would be one of timing if events in West Africa were anything to go by. The real conflict would arise when the conservative estimates of the Administering Authority were challenged by African politicians and trade union leaders. They would be jointly pressing for political and economic independence on a time scale and under a Constitution acceptable to them.

From my own limited perspective the development of a trade union movement in parallel with local political parties seemed inevitable. Trade union legislation was already on the statute, the I.L.O. Convention on Freedom of Association had already been ratified by the Administering Authority and the right to strike was enshrined in the Trades Union Ordinance which I was studying with a view to passing my law examination. Against this background it seemed odd to me that the activities of local trade unions were regarded by the police as an irrelevance. The fact that the Railway African Union had the capacity and the legal right to bring the whole railway system to a complete standstill in a dispute over wages and terms of service was not seen as a likely possibility. I had made a point of getting to know local African trade union officials of whom the Branch Secretary of the Railway African Workers Union was doubtless the most important Other trade union officials represented the Teachers Union, the Transport and General and the Domestic Workers. All seemed fairly friendly and would from time to time visit the Department in connection with complaints or disputes affecting their members, or seeking advice on labour laws.

So far as their effectiveness was concerned all suffered through lack of financial support being directly dependent on the modest subscriptions of their members. It was evident that they all had fairly close links with the main African political party which, like them, was struggling for recognition and support. The relationship between these organizations had considerable potential, if properly organized, and it seemed to me that it was simply a matter of time before effective leadership would emerge calling for political independence from the Administrative Authorities. In the Gold Coast of West Africa the united efforts of the trade union movement and the main political party led by Nkruma had produced an irresistible campaign for full independence. It struck me as strange that the Security Committee appeared to regard these developments as being of little significance. No one seemed to know the names of the local trade union officials or to have any interest in their activities.

Aron, who had good working relationships with local trade union officials alerted me to the impending arrival in Dodoma of the General Secretary of the Railway African Workers Union, a Mr. Tumbo. This official had a formidable reputation as a powerful negotiator in disputes with the Railway Authorities and was highly regarded by African workers. I asked Aron to keep me informed of any developments in connection with this visit and to let it be known that I would be interested in meeting Mr. Tumbo should an opportunity occur during his visit. Late one afternoon Tumbo suddenly appeared at the Department and was introduced by Aron who seemed to be in awe of him. He was quite a striking figure, obviously a Muslim, and very smartly turned out in a clean white Kanzu, an elaborately embroidered Kofia (hat) and sandals. I was expecting a much older man but he seemed to be about 30 years old, tall and slim. With a pleasant open countenance, a friendly smile and a good command of English.

Having settled him comfortably in my office I told Panjawani that we must not be disturbed and we were soon involved in a general discussion about trade union developments and the purpose of Mr. Tumbo's visit to Dodoma. His main purpose was to inspect the Branch Office and address a meeting of local trade union members with the emphasis on increasing union membership. As the office was about to close and I was unable to offer him any refreshment I invited him home and having introduced him to Wyn, who quickly produced afternoon tea, we were able to carry on our discussion. His special concern was a claim he was submitting for increased rates of overtime and his proposals for a training programme to allow his members to qualify as drivers – posts normally reserved for non-Africans. He also expressed an interest in securing some form of assistance to meet the costs of a training programme for Branch Officials – particularly Treasurers. I had to explain that that my Department had no funds for either of these projects but suggested that he might consider sending a carefully drafted Project Proposal to the International Department of the British Trades Union Congress. This might request funding for training and for Fellowships for his members to attend one of the T.U.C. Courses for overseas trade union officials. I suggested that, if he thought it would help, I would be willing to prepare a draft application for his consideration. He accepted this suggestion with alacrity and at the end of our discussions Christopher, as he wished to be called, went through to Wyn to say goodbye and to thank her for her hospitality. After he had left Wyn and I were at a loss to understand how this pleasant and friendly character, who gave the impression of a confident well mannered under graduate, had gained such an unfavorable reputation. It turned out that he was a great admirer of Tom Mboya, the then General Secretary of the Kenya Federation of Labour, and that he hoped to establish himself in a similar position in Tanganyika. The received wisdom amongst the expatriate community, particular those employed with the railways, was that Tumbo was dangerous, rabble rousing troublemaker with an illdisguised hatred of Europeans. Some

were astonished to learn that we had had him as a house guest
and seemed to think that this was really letting the side down.

That evening at Tumbo's invitation I attended what he described
as a mass meeting of trade unionists at the Community Centre.
This turned out to be a new experience for me as Tumbo
introduced me as his rafiki (friend) and I was placed at his right
hand side on the top table. Regrettably my swahili was not really
up to following the proceedings in detail but two things became
immediately apparent. Tumbo was an impressive and persuasive
speaker and that he was held in high regard and some awe by his
many supporters. In the course of his speech the Serikali
(Government) and the Railway Authorities came in for a
battering so too did the Wahindi (Asians) and the Wazungu
(Europeans). He contended that there was no reason why the
railways should not be run at all levels by Africans and that the
sooner that this happened the better. During questions from the
floor things seemed to get pretty noisy and emotional but he was
well able to keep control and the meeting concluded in good order
with a short prayer and much applause.

At the next Security Committee meeting the visit of Mr. Tumbo
was mentioned in a brief report read out by the Special Branch
representative. This indicated the date and time of his arrival by
train, the names of the people who met him, the time of his arrival
at the unions Branch Office and the names of people who called
to see him. It also gave the time of his visit to the Labour
Department, the duration of his stay and the time he
subsequently spent at my house. It concluded by referring to the
meeting at the Community Centre, the names of the people on the
platform (including myself) but offered no comment on what was
discussed. This report was received without comment by the
members, other than the District Commissioner confirming that
he had granted the Union permission to hold the meeting at the
Centre. In the absence of any other comment the Provincial
Commissioner asked if I would like to say a word or two about
this visit. To which I responded by summarizing my impressions
as set out above. The Police Superintendent remained silent but
managed to convey his dissatisfaction with the whole episode. I

gave an account of Mr. Tumbo's visit in my next Report to Labour
Headquarters under the heading Industrial Relations but this too
evoked no comment. During earlier meetings of the Committee
there had been some mention of the events in Kenya where the
Mau Mau situation had caused the Administration to declare a
State of Emergency. In the early 1950s thousands of Kikuyu
tribesmen were living inside Tanganyika's borders, mostly in the
Northern Province. It was known that Mau Mau oaths had been
administered in Moshi and the Kikuyu involved had been
arrested and charged but were released on Appeal. Following the
release of the offenders, the witnesses who had given evidence
against them were murdered. Intelligence reports revealed that
the Mau Mau supporters in the Northern Province planned to
massacre all Europeans on Christmas eve and to burn down all
garages and destroy telephone lines to isolate the area. The
Governor, Sir Edward Twining, promptly initiated an emergency
plan of action summoning all leaders of the Administration to
Lushoto and directed that security organisations, the Kings
African Rifles and the Police Mobile Units be deployed in Moshi
and Arusha. He also declared a State of Emergency in
Tanganyika at midnight on 24th December, 1954. Over 600
known Kikuyu activists were arrested which led to the families of
suspected informers being murdered. The Governor's response
was the rounding up of 15,000 Kikuyu who were screened and
those charged repatriated to Kenya under escort. In response an
armed band of Kikuyu crossed the border from Kenya and
penetrated as far south as Meru. Reacting to this new crisis the
Administration enlisted the support of loyal tribesmen and the
Masai, who have always regarded the Kikuyu as their natural
enemies. The later polished up their spears and very quickly
rounded up or killed the Mau Mau insurgents. Since all this
happened only six or seven months earlier and was only 180 miles
north of Dodoma, it struck me as rather odd that the Security
Committee should be operating on the basis that the primary
security threat should be seen as the dubious machinations of a
handful of foreign Marxists. Recent events in North and West
Africa indicated that, at least in those countries, the main
security threat came from the actions of indigenous 'freedom
fighters' trying to accelerate the pace at which independence

might be gained. It seemed to me that there could be no grounds for assuming that Tanganyika would be exceptional in this respect.

ASSIGNED TO WESTERN PROVINCE

I had settled down into a fairly satisfactory routine running the Department, carrying out a regular safari and inspection programme and dealing confidently with all the routine issues likely to arise in a Provincial Labour Department. I continued to submit my regular reports to Headquarters in Dar es Salaam, but these evoked no acknowledgement or comment and it was easy to assume that I was corresponding with outer space. Since taking up my assignment, Headquarters had only been in contact with me on three issues, a letter advising me that I had been allocated a vehicle and driver (which arrived some days after the driver himself arrived). Then a telephone call to advise me that my son Peter would be arriving by plane that day and finally, a letter advising me that my car loan application had been approved. As a newly appointed officer I found this slightly odd but it was obviously preferable to being chased about every minor detail and I operated on the assumption that no news was good news and that thus far my efforts had not evoked any queries or adverse comments.

Suddenly this all changed when I received a long and detailed letter directing me to assume the duties of Labour Officer, Western Province, forthwith but at the same time to continue my duties as Labour Officer, Central Province. In practice this involved my making regular journeys on the Central Line trains (about 200 miles) to Tabora, the Provincial headquarters of the Western Province, and assuming responsibility for the staff and operations of the Department. It turned out that the officer whose duties I was to assume had been dismissed at short notice and I was to replace him on a temporary basis until the post could be filled by a substantive officer. I found Tabora to be almost a replica of Dodoma in the sense that the Provincial Headquarters was located in an old German 'Boma' alongside the Central railway line. The Township was larger than Dodoma, divide into

European, Asian and African quarters and there was a substantial bazaar area made up mainly of Asian 'dukas'.

On first reporting to the Provincial Commissioner I got a fairly cool reception and this was repeated by other senior officials with whom I made contact. This struck me as pretty odd especially as I had a similar reception from the staff at the Labour Department. It transpired, however, that the officer I was replacing had been very popular and most people were of the opinion that his prosecution and dismissal over alleged false mileage claims was unjustified. The Labour department staff were very similar to those in Dodoma except that they were all members of the predominant tribe the Wanyemwezi. I had to find accommodation at the Railway Hotel during my visits and I was given a special pass authorizing my travel on any train service between Tabora and Dodoma. This gave rise to some odd experiences as the mixed–goods and goods trains had no dining car or sleeping accommodation so I traveled with the Guard in the Caboose at the end of the train. The Guards were usually Sikhs or Hindu who only had food for themselves and the water, which was taken on board at various stops along the line was not to be trusted.

This assignment lasted two months covering six visits to Tabora and it was fairly tricky as at one stage I had to settle a strike by railway bus drivers. It was a relief to get back to my routine duties back in Dodoma. However, I had no sooner settled down to my normal duties when I received yet another surprising letter from Headquarters. This informed me that a new post of 'Labour Officer, Personal Assistant', had been created at Headquarters in Dar es Salaam and that I was to take up this appointment forthwith. From the limited information available it appeared that I was to be personal assistant to the Labour Commissioner and that the post was demanding in the sense that I would be expected to undertake staff work on all aspects of the Commissioner's duties. Given my very limited experience I was at a loss to understand why I had been selected for such a post and my first worry was what impact this might have on my ability to pass my language and law examinations. I was also conscious

of the fact that I greatly enjoyed the freedom and independence
typical of a Provincial appointment. Although staff work itself
would present few problems, given that I had served a few years
as Adjutant in my military service, a 9 to 5 desk job was not what
I had envisaged when I sought a Colonial Service appointment.
On the other hand, so far as Wyn and the children were
concerned, this transfer to the big city was not without interest.
The children would doubtless find better schools and there would
be far better food choices and other commodities not typically
available in up-country stations plus access to improved health
services. Access to the golden sands and palm fringed beaches of
the Indian Ocean, only glimpsed in passing when we first arrived
in Dar es Salaam, seemed to be uppermost in the childrens minds
when the transfer proposition was put to them. Their only real
concern was that we should take the servants with us.

LEAVING DODOMA

My replacement turned out to be a newly appointed officer who, before being employed by the Labour Department, had served for eight years in the Public Works Department. It quickly became apparent that the hand-over was not going to be a happy experience since he chose to speak almost exclusively in Swahili, a language in which he was extremely proficient. He also seemed to consider that there was very little that I could tell him since his eight years service (albeit at a lower grade) against my 12 months put him at a decided advantage. Introducing him to the staff and handing over the accounts and stores turned out to be something of a monologue since my observations and advice were received in almost complete and disinterested silence. In response to my asking if every thing was all right his only comment was "well, obviously there will have to be some radical changes". When asked what exactly he had in mind he replied "I would have thought that they would be blindingly obvious". Against this unpromising background I thought it best to concentrate on drafting a comprehensive set of handing over notes but couldn't resist the feeling that they would be completely ignored.

Wyn seemed to encounter a similar situation in trying to welcome the new officer's wife. It seems that in some elements of the Colonial Service it is often the case that the wife takes on the same seniority as her husband and Wyn's attempts to introduce her to the local Asian shop-keepers and to our neighbours was thought to be completely unnecessary. This was pretty worrying and we were both beginning to feel that there may be something wrong with the way we were going about things. However, subsequent events put our minds at rest since the officer concerned proved to be completely unsuitable and had his services terminated at short notice.

Leaving Dodoma was not without some sadness. We had made some good friends who we would miss and I would certainly miss my work and the staff at the Department. Similarly, Wyn would miss her pupils and friends at the Aga Khan School and we would certainly miss our servants with whom we had a good working relationship. The reaction of our friends to our transfer to Dar es Salaam were fairly mixed since it was the ambition of most officers and their wives to secure a posting to the Capital. In career terms it was obviously desirable to be working in the upper echelons of the various Departments where ones abilities may be noticed and promotion prospects enhanced. They found it perplexing that someone such as myself with only 12 months service should be selected for such an appointment.

With our goods loaded on the train and the house handed over we set out on our safari to Dar-es-Salaam by car, a journey the children were really looking forward to. I couldn't resist calling into the Department for a final goodbye and having shaken every ones hand Maloda walked out to the car with me saying 'Bwana huyu hatutaki' (this new Bwana we don't like).

TRANSFER TO DAR ES SALAAM

Leaving Dodoma was a time for reflection since we had all, the whole family, experienced a great deal that was very different compared to our former life in England. For myself it seemed strange that what was initially a challenging and very uncertain new role, had fairly swiftly become a pleasant, interesting and satisfying experience. In many ways my first 12 months had been a confidence building experience in the sense that I was now comfortable working with Africans and in career terms the prospect of long term service overseas and the possibility of eventual advancement seemed not only acceptable but in many ways attractive. Wyn and the children had found little difficulty in adapting to our new and often strange circumstances and her teaching assignment with Ismaili children had turned out to be particularly interesting and rewarding.

I could only speculate about my new role as Personal Assistant to the Labour Commissioner and my hope was that this would turn out to be real assignment and that I should not be seen as the Headquarters 'go for'. It seemed pretty obvious that I was going to miss the independence, freedom of action and opportunities for safari, which I enjoyed as a Provincial Labour Officer. Staff work was not particularly challenging as my experience as Adjutant was sufficient to ensure that I might reasonably expect to perform such duties without special difficulty. However, the prospect of a desk bound 9am to 5pm office appointment in an urban environment might prove less attractive than the post I had just vacated. On the other hand, a glance at the Staff List showed that in terms of seniority there were 14 officers ahead of me, some with over 10 years service, so prospects for advancement in the Labour Department were less than encouraging. In Dar es Salaam, however, I would be working in close contact with major Departments such as the Treasury and the Secretariat and would thus be aware of any promotion opportunities which may materialize and for which I may be eligible to apply. Reflecting on my general impressions of working closely with Africans over a period of 12 months I wondered what conclusions might be drawn. One thing which was particularly noticeable was when unusual situations occurred, which called for imagination or initiative the teams reactions were often fairly negative. Aron, perhaps due to his military training, was very good at carrying out specific tasks once he had been told what to do and he could organise the team very effectively but he would seldom put forward a suggestion. Abdullah saw his role as simply that of a driver, so long as the truck started he would drive and do that competently always remembering to check oil, petrol, tyre pressures and water. But if there was a problem starting the engine, or if it stopped for some reason, he would in effect 'switch off' being content to pass the problem to someone else or, in the final analysis, see this as the will of Alah and accept it with resignation. The Messengers were content to take the later view in most situations their reaction to most unforeseen things being 'Bahati Mbaya' – bad luck, without ruling out the possibility of witchcraft, or simply 'Shauri ya Mungu' – an act of God.

Wondering why this should be, I was reminded of the situations deliberately created by the Directing Staff when I attended the War Office Selection Board set up to determine ones suitability for a Commission. A group of 14 candidates with no name or rank, other than a large identifying number pinned on their backs, would be set a problem and, without appointing a leader, be told to get on with it. The problem such as climbing a very high wall and then crossing a deep river with a limited amount of equipment such as ropes (usually too short) or planks (too thin to carry much weight) and a couple of barrels. All 14 candidates would be aware that the Directing Staff were watching to see who would emerge as the natural leader of the group. There would then follow scene in which all kinds of orders would be given by individual candidates, usually ignored by the rest of the group and eventually various solutions would be attempted often with dire results. The whole point was that it seemed natural to assume that all sorts of initiatives would emerge in response to the problem set.   Working with the team, when confronted with problems initiatives or suggestions were mostly absent.   Since there was often no lack of intelligence, although many were under educated through no fault of their own, it was a matter of speculation why this should be.   It occurred to me that the tribal cultural environment might be a major factor since tribalism is based largely on subjection to the absolute authority of the Paramount Chief, Chiefs, Clan Leaders etc.   Conformity with tribal behaviour patterns is rigidly enforced and breaches of taboos firmly dealt with.   Even the timing of planting crops and subsequent harvesting requires the permission of Chiefs or Sub-Chiefs and the right to clear bush and occupy land (which is tribally owned) requires prior approval.

This analysis suddenly collapsed around my ears as I remembered Mr. Johnathan and his all African football team. Watching them play all the uncertainties outlined above seem to fall away, anticipation, teamwork, rapid reaction to quickly changing play and individual initiatives were all a natural part of their game. So, with these thoughts in mind and after a long, hot, dusty journey our spirits rose as we finally caught sight of Dar es Salaam in the distance. Its palm fringed harbour, golden beaches and small offshore islands in the brilliant blue sea of the Zanzibar Channel, certainly offered an inviting perspective compared with semi-desert conditions of the Central Province.

EPILOGUE

Glynn passed his Advanced Level Kiswahili and Law Exams and was eventually confirmed in his appointment. During his service in Labour Headquarters he was appointed as Secretary to three major Commissions concerned with Wages and Conditions in the Sisal Industry, the Rationalisation of the Tanganyike Ports and Dock Labour and the Territorial Minimum Wages Board. He was also directly involved in the Anglo / Belgian Review of Migrant Labour in Ruanda-Urundi and with the Wittwatersrand Native Labour Review in Southern Rhodesia. He was promoted to a higher grade post in the Treasury and promoted to a Super Scale post in the Prime Minister's Office. Following Independence he was appointed Staff Development Adviser in the Office of the President financed by the Ford Foundation. At the request of the Botswana Government he was seconded to the post of Staff Development Consultant in the President's Office in Gaborone and simultaneously became Head of the Ford Foundation's Aid Programme for Southern Africa... Finally, he was appointed Senior Adviser on Employment aspects of British Aid Policy in the Foreign and Commonwealth Office in London. His service to development in Africa was formally recognised by the award of the OBE by H.M. The Queen in 1974 and the award of the Presidential Order of Merit by the President of Botswana, Sir Seretse Khama, in 1978.

List of Photographs and Paintings

Printed in the United Kingdom
by Lightning Source UK Ltd.
104160UKS00001B/322-327